Concert in the Kitchen

This cookbook is a collection of favorite recipes, which are not necessarily original recipes.

Friends of Portland Symphony Orchestra
P.O. Box 3573
Portland, Maine 04104
(207) 773-6128

Cover Painting: Flowers on Stove
Alfred C. Chadbourn, 1997
Back Cover Photograph: Portland Head Light

Library of Congress Number: 99-072958
ISBN: 0-9601266-2-7

Edited, Designed and Manufactured by
Favorite Recipes® Press
An imprint of

FRP

P.O. Box 305142, Nashville, Tennessee 37230
(800) 358-0560

Designers: Brad Whitfield and Susan Breining
Art Director: Steve Newman
Project Manager: Linda Bennie

Manufactured in the United States of America
First Printing: 2000   10,000 copies

Concert in the Kitchen

A Medley of Maine Recipes
Orchestrated by Friends of Portland Symphony Orchestra

Foreword

Making music and creating a dish, and their inherent similarities,
have fascinated me my whole life. I cannot recall a single important occasion,
or any simple gathering, without both.
Creating a superb cuisine is justly called the culinary art.
Art is, after all, the cause and effect of attuning the senses, whether sight,
hearing, or touch. What are the secrets behind the artistry that allow leading chefs
to compose a brilliant dish or a spectacular menu with the potential to touch
and inspire us in much the same way as the compositions of Beethoven or Mozart?
Food is all too frequently mistaken as being only about taste.
Food is rich with sensory stimuli, not only of taste, but of smell, vision, touch,
sound — and in turn, stirs memories and emotions and cultural connotations.

A great dining experience is more on a par with a great concert experience
than any other artistic activity, each with a rhythm and harmony all its own.
The act of composing in both activities requires the creator to combine parts
into a unified, harmonious whole. In music, the art is in the arranging
of sounds in time to produce a composition that elicits an aesthetic response
in a listener. Great symphonies have inspired and moved the audience to tears.
Why not great food? With a great meal, a single aroma serves up
memories of romantic encounters, personal triumphs, cherished family gatherings,
and sun-soaked days of childhood. A single flavor has the power to suggest
an entire region of the world. The most beautiful symphony of food
I have ever experienced was at the rooftop Japanese restaurant in the Nikko Hotel
in San Francisco. It was a meal that touched my palate, my mind,
and my heart, and left me speechless.

Cooking is one of the simplest and most gratifying of the arts, compared to music making, which can be complicated and intense. Following the recipe is, to me, like realizing the great symphonic score of Beethoven. But in cooking I also find relaxation. The activity gives me pleasure during the process, and ultimate rewards at the end. For the cook, it might also lead to immediate verbal praise, the culinary version of applause.

This cookbook was composed by the Friends of the Portland Symphony Orchestra, in their passion for supporting the PSO. This support has been vital to our orchestra's music making. I am ever grateful to Penny Parson and Marti Lane and all the wonderful people who devoted their precious time to the publication of this masterpiece. I hope this collection of symphonic recipes will create wonderful memories for you. May it enrich your life, just as you will be enriched by the great music of the master composers.

Toshiyuki Shimada
Music Director and Conductor
Portland Symphony Orchestra

About our Artists

ALFRED C. (CHIP) CHADBOURN

Alfred C. (Chip) Chadbourn (1921-1998) was born in Izmir, Turkey. After spending his childhood in France and California, he studied art in Los Angeles and in Paris at the Beaux Arts and La Grande Chaumiere. His first one-man show in Paris in 1949 was patronized by Jean Cocteau. His work was greatly influenced by French impressionism, and he was best known locally for his colorful images of coastal Maine and still lifes of food. His paintings are included in many museums, including the Boston Museum of Fine Arts, Corcoran Gallery of Washington, D.C., Chicago Art Institute, and the Portland Museum of Art, as well as in the private collections of Sir Laurence Olivier, Prince Rainer of Monaco, Jacques Cousteau, Walter Cronkite, and many others. He was a longtime resident of Yarmouth, Maine.

JANET CONLON MANYAN

Janet Conlon Manyan, of Kennebunkport, has a graduate degree in art from Brooklyn College, CUNY. There she received the Charles Shaw Award in Painting. She was awarded the Critic's Grant from the Vermont Studio Center upon the recommendation of Lennart Anderson and has also completed independent study with Alfred Chadbourn. She has exhibited with the Maine Coast Artists, Hera Gallery in Wakefield, Rhode Island, Barn Gallery in Ogunquit and Squbb, and the National Arts Club in New York. Her interest lies in using a small intimate composition to produce a personal connection with the audience.

CHARLES REID

Charles Reid was born in Cambridge, New York and studied art at the
University of Vermont at Montpelier and the Art Students League of New York.
He was awarded the Childe Hassam Purchase Prize at The American Academy of Arts
and Letters in 1975 and 1976. He won awards from the National Academy of Design in
1971-1975 and 1978, from the American Watercolor Society in 1977 and 1978, and from
Allied Artists in 1975. He is an Associate of the National Academy of Design.
In addition to painting, he teaches workshops across the country and has written
five books on painting figures, portraits, and still lifes in oil and watercolor.

SUZANNE HARDEN

Suzanne Harden, from Columbus, Ohio, received her education from Indiana University.
She was an education major and taught school, but her first love was creating
the artwork for her bulletin boards. Her talent blossomed from there.
She began formal art instruction in Ohio and continued at the Maine College of Art.
Suzanne started out doing faux painting in private homes while living in Ohio.
When she moved to Maine, she had the privilege of meeting Alfred Chadbourn who
suggested that she sit down and paint what she saw out her kitchen window.
Suzanne did just that in her painting of "Tulips." She has exhibited with
Bayview Gallery in Portland and Camden, Maine.

Portland Public Market

The idea of the public market as a specific place where products are sold or traded regularly is a customary element of everyday life in many cultures. For example, Europe boasts about 80,000 markets, including at least 3,000 market halls. In the United States, among the first records of market activity in the colonies is a 1634 entry in the diary of Governor Winthrop, showing a court order to establish a market in Boston, which was constructed in the town center leading to the town dock. In Portland the first market hall dates back to 1825. Agricultural trade took place on the ground floor while the building's upper level was used for meetings and other public functions. As the wealth of the city grew, a new facade and elaborate double staircase was added, similar to the design of Fanueil Hall in Boston. When this building was removed in the 1890s, Portland's market customers depended upon the seasonal outdoor farmers' markets, which eventually located in Monument Square and Deering Oaks Park.

However, in 1998, through the insight and generosity of Elizabeth Noyce, noted Maine philanthropist, a new indoor public market was created just a block from the original market building. Constructed with massive Douglas fir timber beams high above glass and brick walls and a two-story-high granite fireplace, it is one of a small coterie of new public markets built in North America since the mid-century. Maine's best foods, fresh from local farmers and food producers, are once again available year-round from independent Maine-owned businesses.

Thank you, Portland Public Market, for being our sponsor.

Steering Committee

Debra Bilodeau
Mary Ann Brennan-Newcomb
Kathy Crispin
Marti Lane
Ellen McCarthy
Penny Parson
Sally Serunian

EDITOR
Marti Lane

CONTENT SELECTION
Kathy Crispin

RESEARCH
Debra Bilodeau

MARKETING
Debra Bilodeau, Peg Furey, Ron Gramaglia, Suzanne Hamlin,
Kathryn Lindsey, Ellen McCarthy, Peter McCarthy, Penny Parson,
Ruth Rose, Sally Serunian, Gail Witherill

TESTING
Connie Batson, Kathy Crispin, Peg Furey, Linda Graffam,
Pat Forsyth, Caroline Pratt

Recipe Contributors

Ben Alfiero

Mrs. M. Bright Alloo

Jean Alvord

Sally Bancroft

Linda Bartlett

Connie Batson

Joyce Bayliss

Paul Bayliss

Vera Berv

Debra Bilodeau

Connie Bingham

Joanne O. Bingham

Mary Ann Brennan-Newcomb

Dory Bridges

Emmy Brown

Stefani Burk

Carolyn Cantrell

Jonathan Cartwright

Carole Case

Michael J. Chitwood

Kathy Crispin

Maxine Duffy

Bob Dyk

Ann Ertman

Judy Flaker

Pat Forsyth

Karen Foster

Katie Freilinger

Vince and Peg Furey

Patricia Burton Ganz

Lawrence Golan

Lynn Goldfarb

Linda L. Graffam

Gloria R. Gramaglia

Captain Alan J. Graves

Gladys Hager

Carol Hale

Lois Hart

Phyllis Hartley

Charles A. Harvey, Jr.

Mark Steven Holt

Nancy MacMillan Johnson

Marti Lane

Mary Larrabee

Jack and Marty MacDiarmid

Larry Matthews, Jr.

Ellen McCarthy

Jean G. McMullan

Katharine Meeker

Charles Miranda

Jane S. Moody

Clorinda Noyes

Joe and Penny Parson

Pam Plumb

Caroline Pratt

John H. Reevy

Mary Morse Reevy

Julie Restuccia

Bonnie M. Riddle

Nancy Whiting Sears

Sally Serunian

Irene Shevenell

Toshiyuki Shimada and

Eva Virsik-Shimada

Donna L. Snyder

Ann E. Spaulding

Judy Stauss

Jessica Stensrud

Joseph B. Stevens

Pamela A. Straw

Nancy B. Thal

Mit Twombly

Julianne Verret

Judith Warren

Laurel Will

Rita Willis

Marcella Wilson

Gail E. Witherill

Joan Woodsum

Preface

Over sixty years ago, a group of leading musicians in Portland, Maine, formed an ensemble that today is known as the Portland Symphony Orchestra, a $2.4 million business that attracts some 90,000 people. Portland is one of the two smallest population bases in the country to support an orchestra of the PSO's size. Under Music Director and Conductor Toshiyuki Shimada, the Portland Symphony Orchestra's 82 contracted players perform nearly 60 concerts a year, plus over 100 small ensemble educational programs. It gives outdoor concerts during the summer in several Maine communities. Maestro Shimada was named to the PSO post in 1986 and is the Orchestra's eleventh conductor.

The Portland Symphony Orchestra's home is Merrill Auditorium, regarded as Maine's premier performance space, seating 1,907 people. A two-year renovation project, completed in 1997, represented a well-orchestrated collaborative effort by the community, the auditorium's primary tenants, a community fund-raising organization called Greater Portland Cares, and Portland's City Council. Merrill Auditorium houses one of only two municipal organs in the country. The 6,613-pipe Kotzschmar Memorial Organ was built and installed by the Austin Organ Company in 1912 through the generosity of Philadelphia publisher Cyrus Curtis, the Portland native who owned the *Saturday Evening Post* and *Ladies Home Journal*.

Friends of the PSO has evolved from the original Women's Auxiliary, which was established under the leadership of Mrs. Guy Gannett in 1932 to support the symphony through fund-raising and sponsorships. Today the Friends are an active volunteer organization of over 200 members, sponsoring Showhouses, Kitchen Tours, and other projects that contribute to the artistic excellence and financial stability of the orchestra. Additionally, the Friends provide volunteer support for the education programs of the PSO and annually award scholarships to promising young musicians in our community. Through these activities and numerous others, the organization continues to generate new interest and enthusiasm for a most important contributor to the cultural life of Portland – the Portland Symphony Orchestra.

Contents

Acknowledgements

Although many people have contributed to the development of this book,
there are some who have worked especially hard to bring this project to fruition.

We are most grateful to Tom Crotty of Frost Gulley Gallery for his generosity and
expertise in helping us select the original artwork contained in this book.
Also, we are grateful to Jay York for helping us with the necessary photography.
Most importantly, it was only through the generosity of the artists, their families, and the
owners of these works (Edgar Beem, Robert and Kathy Crispin, and Richard and
Roberta Wright) that we could offer this visual tribute to Maine cooking.

Special thanks to our fine chefs, Jonathan Cartwright of the White Barn Inn in
Kennebunkport and Larry Matthews, Jr., of the Back Bay Grill for their unique recipes.
Our thanks also to Rob Anderson of The Whip and Spoon and
Jeff Kane of National Distributors, Inc.

Finally, this book would not have been possible without the enthusiasm and support
of our membership, the staff of the Portland Symphony Orchestra,
the orchestra members, and our Maestro, Toshiyuki Shimada.

Introduction

The Portland Symphony Orchestra is celebrating 75 years of orchestra live! – and the Friends of the Portland Symphony Orchestra are pleased to commemorate this event with the publication of our second cookbook, *Concert in the Kitchen*. In keeping with the theme of our past book, which celebrates the uniqueness of Maine cooking, this book contains tried and true recipes from our members and friends.

The purpose of the Friends of the PSO, established in the 1930s as the Women's Committee, is to aid and support the Orchestra through educational programs, fund-raising projects, and volunteer services. Our first cookbook, the *Portland Symphony Cookbook*, was published in 1974 in honor of the orchestra's 50th season, and proceeds from the sale of over 45,000 copies of this book have contributed significantly toward helping to pay the mounting costs of operating a first-rate orchestra. Special thanks must go to Maestro Toshiyuki Shimada for encouraging us to produce an encore to our first book, and to Marti Lane, Kathy Crispin, and Debra Bilodeau for getting this project off the ground.

Concert in the Kitchen is representative of the beauty, culture, and history as well as distinctive cuisine of the state of Maine. From mussels and crab cakes to blueberries and fiddleheads, we hope you will enjoy this harmonious volume of Maine treats.

Penelope G. Parson
President, Friends of the Portland Symphony Orchestra

The Portland Head Light

(pictured on the rear cover)

The Portland Head Light, built in 1791, was commissioned by George Washington.
He ordered masons to use material taken from the fields and shores for the building,
as the government had little money at the time. A keeper's house was built in 1891.
The station has changed little since then except for the replacement of the Fresnel lens
with a modern optic. The light was automated in August, 1989.
Renovation of the keeper's quarters was accomplished in 1990 to create a museum,
which was dedicated in 1992. The town of Cape Elizabeth now operates the museum.
The Portland Head Light is located adjacent to Fort Williams Park.

Just as the lighthouses of Maine represent stability
and certainty in an ever-changing sea, so we hope these recipes
from our community will become a strong point of reference
as you enjoy our Concert in the Kitchen.

Curtain Raiser
Appetizers

Curtain Raiser

Appetizers

Mariner's Dream Potatoes *19*
Toasted Brie Cheese *20*
Pierside Pâté *21*
Scandinavian Meatballs *21*
Clam-Stuffed Mushrooms *22*
Classic Lobster Dip *22*
Mushroom Cheese Puffs *23*
Hors d'Oeuvre Mandala *24*
Mussels Italiano *25*
Horton's Smoked Salmon Pinwheels *26*
Rocky Coast Gravlax *27*
Maine Salmon Fillet Cured in Dill and Citrus Marinade *28*
Smoked Salmon Tortilla Bites *29*
Seared Maine Diver Scallops with Roasted Corn Salsa *30*
Greek Blintzes *31*
Tomato, Avocado, Corn and Black Bean Salsa *32*
Smoked Trout with Horseradish Cream *33*
Pickled Antipasto *34*

Mariner's Dream Potatoes

Yield: 24 servings

12	small red or white new potatoes	1/2	cup sour cream and/or plain yogurt
2	tablespoons milk or light cream		
•	Salt and pepper to taste	4	ounces (or more) red and/or black caviar
2	tablespoons (1/4 stick) butter, melted		

Arrange the potatoes on a baking sheet. Bake at 400 degrees for 30 minutes or just until tender. Let stand to cool.

Cut each potato into halves. Scoop out the potato, leaving a shell. Mash the potato pulp with the milk, salt and pepper in a bowl. Brush the potato shells with the butter. Bake at 450 degrees for 10 minutes or until light brown.

Cook the mashed potato mixture in the microwave just until heated through. Fill each shell with a spoonful of the mashed potato mixture. Add a dollop of the sour cream. Top with a spoonful of caviar. Serve immediately.

Note: May substitute chopped vegetables such as scallions or sweet peppers for the caviar. May sprinkle the potatoes with grated cheese and bacon bits.

Toasted Brie Cheese

Yield: 10 servings

1/2	teaspoon chili powder	1	(1-pound) loaf round bread
1/2	teaspoon dry mustard	1	tablespoon butter, softened
1/2	teaspoon garlic powder	1	(8-ounce) round Brie cheese
1/2	teaspoon sugar		

Combine the chili powder, dry mustard, garlic powder and sugar in a small bowl and mix well.

Cut a round slice the same diameter and depth as the Brie from the top of the bread, leaving a shell and reserving the bread slice. Spread the butter over the inside of the bread. Sprinkle 1 teaspoon of the chili powder mixture over the butter. Cut 2-inch slits 1 inch apart around the cut edge of the bread.

Remove the rind from the Brie. Place the Brie in the center of the bread. Sprinkle with the remaining chili powder mixture. Top with the reserved bread slice. Place the bread round on a baking sheet. Bake at 350 degrees for 20 to 30 minutes or until the Brie is heated through.

Remove the bread round to a serving plate. Take the top off the bread round and break into small pieces. Serve with the Brie.

Pierside Pâté

Yield: 16 servings

8	ounces fresh chicken livers	1/4	teaspoon dry mustard
4	ounces fresh mushrooms, sliced	1/4	teaspoon rosemary
1/4	cup chopped scallions	1/4	teaspoon dill
1/2	teaspoon salt	1	garlic clove, minced
2	tablespoons (1/4 stick) butter	1/2	cup (1 stick) butter, softened
1/3	cup dry white wine		

Sauté the chicken livers, mushrooms, scallions and salt in 2 tablespoons butter in a skillet for 5 minutes. Stir in the wine, dry mustard, rosemary, dill and garlic. Simmer, covered, for 10 minutes. Cook, uncovered, until the liquid has evaporated.

Spoon the mixture into a food processor or blender container. Add 1/2 cup butter. Process until of the desired consistency. Spoon into a crock. Chill, covered, for 8 hours or longer before serving.

Scandinavian Meatballs

Yield: 24 meatballs

3	tablespoons finely chopped onion	1/3	cup bread crumbs
2	to 3 tablespoons butter	1	pound ground beef
1/2	cup water	1	egg
1/2	cup cream	1 1/2	teaspoons salt
		1/4	teaspoon pepper

Sauté the onion in the butter in a skillet until golden brown. Remove the onion with a slotted spoon to a small bowl, reserving the butter in the skillet.

Whisk the water and cream in a bowl. Add the bread crumbs. Let stand until the bread crumbs have absorbed the liquid. Add the ground beef, onion, egg, salt and pepper and mix well. Shape into bite-size balls. Cook the meatballs in the reserved butter in the skillet until brown on all sides; drain. May serve with a favorite sauce.

Clam-Stuffed Mushrooms

Yield: 36 servings

36 large mushrooms	1/4 teaspoon salt
1/3 cup butter	• Freshly ground pepper to taste
16 ounces clams, minced, rinsed, drained	2 garlic cloves, minced
3 tablespoons sliced scallions, white part only	3/4 cup mayonnaise
2 tablespoons chopped fresh parsley	1/2 teaspoon prepared mustard

Remove the stems from the mushrooms, leaving the caps intact. Chop the stems. Sauté the mushroom stems in the butter in a skillet for 10 minutes. Add the clams, scallions, parsley, salt, pepper and garlic and mix well. Sauté for 5 minutes.

Stuff the mushroom caps with the clam mixture. Arrange in a lightly greased 9x13-inch baking pan. Combine the mayonnaise and mustard in a small bowl and mix well. Top each of the mushrooms with a small amount of the mayonnaise mixture. May refrigerate, covered, until ready to bake.

Bake at 350 degrees for 10 to 15 minutes or until heated through.

Classic Lobster Dip

Yield: 32 servings

1 cup sour cream	2 teaspoons curry powder
1 cup plain yogurt	8 ounces chopped fresh or thawed frozen lobster meat
2 scallions, thinly sliced	
1 tablespoon fresh lemon juice	

Combine the sour cream, yogurt, scallions, lemon juice and curry powder in a bowl and mix until smooth. Stir in the lobster.

Refrigerate, covered, for 1 hour or longer. May be served with fresh vegetables or toasted bread rounds.

Mushroom Cheese Puffs

Yield: 24 puffs

3 ounces cream cheese, softened
1 (2-ounce) can mushrooms, drained, chopped
2 tablespoons chopped pimento
1 teaspoon instant minced onion, or 1 tablespoon chopped fresh onion

2 drops of Tabasco sauce
1 (8-count) can crescent rolls
1/2 cup chopped walnuts

Combine the cream cheese, mushrooms, pimento, onion and Tabasco sauce in a bowl and mix well.

Separate the crescent roll dough into 4 rectangles, pressing the perforations to seal.

Spread each rectangle with 1/4 of the mushroom mixture. Roll as for a jelly roll, beginning at the long end and sealing the seam.

Cut each roll into 6 slices. Coat each slice with the walnuts. Arrange on a baking sheet.

Bake at 375 degrees for 15 minutes or until golden brown. Serve warm.

LOBSTER NUTRITIONAL DATA

	Cholesterol (mg)	Calories	Saturated Fat (g)
Lobster (boiled, 3 1/2 oz.)	72	98	0.1
Skinless Chicken	85	173	1.3
Skinless Turkey	86	140	0.4
Eggs (2)	550	158	3.4

Hors d'Oeuvre Mandala

Yield: 12 servings

This makes a beautiful presentation; it really looks like a mandala.

1 (9-inch) frozen pastry shell, thawed

12 ounces cream cheese, softened

2 ounces bleu cheese (optional)

1/2 cup mayonnaise

1/2 teaspoon onion salt or sesame salt

7 cherry tomatoes, cut into halves

4 or 5 fresh mushrooms, sliced

• Chopped parsley sprigs

1 hard-cooked egg, chopped

2 or 3 pitted olives, sliced

Pat the pastry into an 11-inch circle on a baking sheet. Prick the pastry all over with a fork. Bake at 425 degrees for 8 minutes or until light brown. Let stand to cool. Place on a serving platter.

Beat the cream cheese, bleu cheese, mayonnaise and onion salt in a mixer bowl until light and fluffy. Spread evenly over the crust. Refrigerate, covered, for 4 hours or longer.

Arrange the tomatoes, mushrooms, parsley, egg and olives in a series of circles, starting at the outer edge in the order listed and overlapping ingredients when necessary. Cut into wedges to serve.

Mussels Italiano

Yield: 12 servings

2   pounds mussels
1   cup chianti or other dry
    red wine

2   (14-ounce) cans chopped
    tomatoes with Italian herbs
    and garlic

Scrub the mussels and remove the beards.

Combine the chianti and tomatoes in a stockpot, stirring to mix. Add the mussels.

Bring to a boil over high heat. Reduce the heat to medium-low. Simmer for 10 minutes or until the mussels open, stirring frequently. Discard any unopened mussels. Serve immediately with Italian bread.

MUSICAL NOTES OF INTEREST

Although we often think that the practice of enjoying music with meals is modern, in reality it is quite old. Izaak Walton in his Compleat Angler *in exalting fish writes, "The Romans at the height of their glory...had music to usher in their sturgeons, lampreys, and mullets." The great sixteenth century British explorer, Sir Francis Drake, reportedly carried expert musicians on his voyages. A Spanish captain taken prisoner by Drake wrote in his diary, "He has all possible luxuries...He dines and sups to the music of viols." The tradition continued in America where Judge Samuel Sewall, the famous New Englander, reported an incident at the Council Dinner in Boston in his diary, "Had no musick, though the Lieut. Govr. had promised it." By the twentieth century, the London caterers, Messrs. Lyons, were employing 300 musicians in thirty orchestras at an annual cost of over 150,000 pounds to play at their various establishments. Although the restaurant orchestra is now a thing of the past, recorded music is still considered an integral part of fine dining.*

Horton's Smoked Salmon Pinwheels

Yield: 32 to 40 servings

For a beautiful presentation, serve these pinwheels on a dark-colored plate.

6 ounces cream cheese, softened
1/2 teaspoon finely grated orange zest
1/2 teaspoon finely grated lemon zest
2 teaspoons green peppercorns, crushed

1/2 teaspoon freshly chopped thyme
2 tablespoons freshly chopped chives
8 ounces Horton's Smoked Atlantic Salmon, sliced

Mix the cream cheese, orange zest, lemon zest, peppercorns, thyme and chives in a bowl. Spread in a thin layer over each of the salmon slices. Roll as for a jelly roll. Refrigerate, covered, until firm.

Cut into 1/4-inch slices and secure with wooden picks. Arrange on a plate. Garnish with lemon slices or parsley.

A great find in the Portland Public Market is smoked seafood. It is a wonderful delicacy, readily turning a simple salad, omelet, or pasta dish into an intriguing gourmet experience. Naturally smoked seafood using cold spring water, a little salt, and lots of natural smoke from hardwoods is a specialty of Horton's of Waterboro.

Rocky Coast Gravlax

Yield: 8 to 10 servings

2   (1- to 1¼-pound) salmon fillets, skin intact
¼   cup salt
2   to 4 tablespoons sugar
2½ teaspoons freshly ground pepper
4   to 6 bunches fresh dill
•   Mustard Sauce

Remove any remaining bones from the fillets and pat dry; do not rinse or scale. Combine the salt, sugar and pepper in a bowl and mix well. Rub the fillets with a small amount of the salt mixture.

Divide the dill into 3 equal portions. Cover the bottom of a deep bowl with 1 portion of the dill. Place 1 fillet skin side down on the bed of dill. Spread a thick layer of the salt mixture over the fillet. Cover with 1 portion of the dill. Spread a layer of the salt mixture over the dill. Add the other fillet skin side up with the thick side against the thin side of the lower fillet. Spread the remaining salt mixture over the fillet. Top with the remaining dill. Cover the layers with a plate or other flat item and a heavy weight, pressing the layers together.

Refrigerate for 1 to 3 days, turning the layers 1 or more times and basting every 12 hours with the resulting liquid. Remove the fillets from the bowl. Cut cross grain into thin slices. Arrange on a serving plate. Serve with the Mustard Sauce.

Mustard Sauce

1   tablespoon wine vinegar
3   tablespoons olive oil
½   teaspoon salt
•   Pepper to taste
3   tablespoons prepared mustard
3   tablespoons sugar
3   tablespoons finely chopped fresh dill

Combine the vinegar, olive oil, salt and pepper in a bowl and mix well. Stir in the mustard, sugar and dill.

Maine Salmon Fillet Cured in Dill and Citrus Marinade

Yield: 32 servings

This is a keeper from the kitchen of Chef Jonathan Cartwright of the
Relais & Chateaux-rated White Barn Inn in Kennebunkport. It is one of his
favorite preparations for Maine salmon.

2	ounces sea salt	1	tablespoon olive oil
1/4	cup sugar	2	oranges
2	juniper berries, crushed	2	lemons
1/2	teaspoon crushed pepper	1	ounce gin
2	pounds boneless Maine salmon fillet, skin intact	1	bunch dill, chopped

Combine the sea salt, sugar, juniper berries and pepper in a bowl and mix well.

Rub the salmon with the olive oil. Place in a shallow pan. Cover with the sea salt mixture.

Peel the oranges and lemons. Arrange the peels over the sea salt mixture. Squeeze the juice of 1 of the oranges and the 2 lemons into a bowl. Stir in the gin. Pour over the peels.

Refrigerate, covered, for 12 to 24 hours. Remove the salmon to a cutting board. Coat with the dill. Cut into slices. Serve on a bed of cucumber with yogurt dressing and toast.

Smoked Salmon Tortilla Bites

Yield: 36 bites

Look for flavored tortillas to use in this recipe. They are better than plain if you can find them!

8	ounces cream cheese, softened	1/4	teaspoon grated orange zest
2	tablespoons chopped fresh cilantro	3/4	teaspoon ground cumin
1	tablespoon minced jalapeño pepper	6	(8-inch) cilantro-flavor or plain flour tortillas
1 1/2	teaspoons grated lime zest	10	ounces smoked salmon, sliced

Beat the cream cheese, cilantro, jalapeño pepper, lime zest, orange zest and cumin in a mixer bowl until well blended. Spread 3 tablespoonfuls of the cream cheese mixture evenly over each tortilla.

Divide the salmon into 6 equal portions. Arrange 1 portion of salmon over the bottom half of each tortilla.

Roll the tortillas up tightly, starting at the bottom. Cut diagonally into 1-inch slices, discarding the end pieces. Arrange on a serving plate. Garnish with fresh cilantro sprigs. Refrigerate, covered, until ready to serve.

Seared Maine Diver Scallops with Roasted Corn Salsa

Yield: 12 servings

- 2   pounds large diver scallops
- •   Salt and pepper to taste
- •   Canola oil
- •   Roasted Corn Salsa

Season the scallops on both sides with salt and pepper. Heat a skillet over high heat until very hot. Add a small amount of canola oil. Add the scallops and sear on both sides. Serve immediately with the Roasted Corn Salsa.

Roasted Corn Salsa

- 3   ears fresh corn
- 8   ounces tomatillos, chopped
- 2   bunches fresh cilantro, chopped
- 1/2   red onion, finely chopped
- •   Lime juice to taste
- •   Salt and pepper to taste

Place the corn on a grill rack over hot coals. Grill on all sides until tender; some charring may occur. Cut the corn off the cob. Combine the corn, tomatillos, cilantro, onion, lime juice, salt and pepper in a bowl and mix well.

Greek Blintzes

Yield: 60 blintzes

This hors d'oeuvre never fails to draw raves.

16 ounces cream cheese, softened
8   ounces creamed cottage cheese
8   ounces feta cheese
2   tablespoons grated Romano
    cheese
3   eggs
2   egg yolks
2   tablespoons onion flakes

2   tablespoons (1/4 stick) butter
1   (10-ounce) package frozen
    chopped spinach, thawed,
    drained
1   (16-ounce) package frozen phyllo
    dough, thawed
•   Melted butter

Beat the cream cheese, cottage cheese, feta cheese, Romano cheese, eggs and egg yolks in a mixer bowl until well mixed.

Sauté the onion flakes in 2 tablespoons butter in a skillet until brown. Stir in the spinach. Sauté for 2 to 3 minutes or until the spinach begins to wilt. Let stand to cool. Add to the cream cheese mixture and mix well.

Unroll the phyllo. Remove 2 sheets, covering the remaining phyllo with waxed paper and a damp towel. Brush the top of the 2 sheets of phyllo with melted butter. Cut with kitchen scissors into 6 rectangles of equal size. Place a heaping teaspoonful of the spinach mixture at the narrow end of each rectangle. Fold the sides over and roll as for a jelly roll, starting at the end with the filling. Repeat the procedure with the remaining phyllo and spinach mixture.

Place the blintzes on a baking sheet. Brush with melted butter. Bake at 350 degrees for 25 minutes or until brown. Serve hot.

Note: The blintzes will keep for several months in the freezer. Arrange unbaked blintzes in layers separated by waxed paper in a freezer-safe container. As needed, remove the desired amount from the freezer and bake as directed.

Tomato, Avocado, Corn and Black Bean Salsa

Yield: 8 ($^1/_2$-cup) servings

2 large tomatoes, finely chopped	$^1/_2$ ripe avocado, minced
$^1/_2$ small red or white onion, minced, rinsed	1 tablespoon fresh lime juice
	• Kernels of 1 ear sweet white corn
1 or 2 jalapeño peppers, or 2 or 3 serrano chiles, seeded, minced (optional)	$^1/_4$ cup chopped fresh cilantro
	1 cup cooked black beans, rinsed, drained

Mix the tomatoes, onion, jalapeño peppers, avocado, lime juice, corn, cilantro and black beans in a bowl. Let stand for 20 minutes. May be refrigerated, covered, for several hours.

Note: May serve as an appetizer with taco chips, as a meal with tortillas or as an accompaniment for grilled chicken breasts or fish.

*The Maine coast is 3,500 miles long with the linear distance
(as the crow flies) being 228 miles.*

Smoked Trout with Horseradish Cream

Yield: 6 servings

1	small head Boston lettuce	3	smoked rainbow trout, skin removed
1	small head radicchio	•	Horseradish Cream
2	heads Belgian endive		

Rinse the Boston lettuce, radicchio and Belgian endive and pat dry. Arrange on 6 salad plates, reserving 6 endive leaves.

Cut the trout into halves. Place 1 portion of trout over the greens on each plate. Arrange 1 reserved endive leaf next to each trout portion, curved side down. Spoon some of the Horseradish Cream onto each of the reserved endive leaf "boats."

Garnish with fresh dill if desired.

Horseradish Cream

3/4	cup whipping cream	•	Salt and pepper to taste
1/2	cup prepared white horseradish, drained		

Whip the cream in a mixer bowl until soft peaks form. Fold in the horseradish. Season with salt and pepper. Refrigerate, covered, until ready to serve.

Note: May add 2 tablespoons chopped fresh dill.

Pickled Antipasto

Yield: 12 to 16 servings

- Flowerets of 1 small head cauliflower
1 green bell pepper, cut into 1/4-inch strips
2 large carrots, cut into 1/4-inch strips
1 large onion, cut into rings
4 ribs celery, cut into 1-inch slices
1 (5-ounce) jar stuffed olives
1 (3-ounce) can button mushrooms
1 (15-ounce) can chick-peas, drained
1 cup vegetable oil
1 1/2 cups wine vinegar
3 tablespoons sugar
1 teaspoon oregano
2 teaspoons salt
- Freshly ground pepper to taste
1 pound mozzarella cheese, sliced
1 pound salami, sliced

Combine the cauliflower, green pepper, carrots, onion, celery, olives, mushrooms and chick-peas in a large bowl and mix well.

Mix the vegetable oil, vinegar, sugar, oregano, salt and pepper in a bowl. Pour over the vegetables, tossing to coat. Refrigerate, covered, for 24 hours or longer, stirring occasionally.

Drain the vegetables. Arrange in the center of a large platter. Arrange the mozzarella cheese and salami around the vegetables. Garnish with parsley.

Note: The marinated vegetables may be served alone as a salad.

Tuning Up

Soups and Salads

Tuning Up

Soups and Salads

Yankee Black Bean Soup

Yield: 10 (1-cup) servings

1	medium onion, chopped	3	(16-ounce) cans black beans
4	garlic cloves, minced	1¹/₂	cups chicken broth
1	tablespoon cumin	3	cups mild or medium salsa
¹/₂	to 1 teaspoon crushed red pepper flakes	2	tablespoons lime juice
2	tablespoons vegetable oil	¹/₂	cup plain yogurt

Sauté the onion, garlic, cumin and red pepper flakes in vegetable oil in a 4-quart stockpot over medium heat for 3 minutes; remove from the heat.

Purée 2 cans undrained black beans with the chicken broth in batches in a food processor. Add to the stockpot. Stir in the remaining undrained black beans, salsa and lime juice. Bring to a boil over medium heat.

Reduce the heat to low. Simmer for 30 minutes. Ladle into soup bowls and top with a dollop of yogurt. Serve hot.

Tipsy Broccoli Cheddar Soup

Yield: 4 servings

3	slices bacon, chopped	1		cup shredded Cheddar cheese
4	scallions, chopped	$1/4$		cup heavy cream
1	rib celery, chopped	$1/4$		teaspoon Tabasco sauce
1	medium carrot, chopped	•		Dash of Worcestershire sauce
$1/4$	cup rolled oats	•		Dash of pepper
$2^1/2$	cups chicken broth	1		cup cooked chopped broccoli
$1/3$	cup dry white wine			

Fry the bacon in a large skillet until crisp. Remove the bacon to paper towels to drain. Drain the skillet, reserving 2 tablespoons of the pan drippings. Add the scallions, celery and carrot. Sauté for 10 minutes or until tender. Stir in the oats, chicken broth and white wine. Bring to a boil and reduce the heat. Simmer for 25 minutes. Cool slightly.

Pour into a food processor or blender container. Process until smooth. Return to the skillet. Bring to a simmer and remove from the heat. Add the Cheddar cheese and stir until the cheese is melted. Add the cream, Tabasco sauce, Worcestershire sauce and pepper. Fold in the broccoli.

Cook over low heat until heated through. Ladle into soup bowls. Sprinkle with the bacon.

Baked Bread and Cabbage Soup

Yield: 4 to 6 servings

1   pound green cabbage, cut into halves, sliced

•   Salt to taste

$1/4$ cup ($1/2$ stick) butter, softened

3   (3x5-inch) $1/2$-inch-thick slices dry white bread, cut into halves

3   (3x5-inch) $1/2$-inch-thick slices dry wheat bread, cut into halves

•   Pepper to taste

2   cups packed coarsely grated fontina cheese

•   Pinch of ground nutmeg

3   cups canned beef broth

Cook the cabbage in boiling salted water to cover in a saucepan for 1 minute or until tender; drain.

Spread butter on both sides of the bread halves. Fry the bread in batches in a skillet over medium heat for 2 minutes on each side or until golden brown.

Arrange $1/2$ of the bread in a 10-cup soufflé dish. Layer $1/2$ of the cabbage over the bread. Sprinkle with salt and pepper. Sprinkle with $1/2$ of the fontina cheese. Repeat the layers. Dot with remaining butter and sprinkle with nutmeg. Pour the beef broth over the layers.

Bake at 350 degrees for 45 minutes or until the top is golden brown. Let stand for 10 minutes. Serve immediately.

Curried Chicken Sprout Soup

Yield: 8 to 10 servings

1	(4-pound) chicken, cut into halves	4	cups coarsely chopped Brussels sprouts
3	quarts water	$1^1/2$	cups chopped ham or Spam
2	medium onions	$1^1/2$	cups chopped tomatoes
3	carrots	$1/2$	cup uncooked rice
1	teaspoon mace	$2^1/2$	tablespoons flour
1	teaspoon salt	$1/4$	cup water
3	tablespoons butter	•	White pepper to taste
1	teaspoon salt	3	hard-cooked eggs, chopped
2	teaspoons curry powder	$1/2$	cup chopped parsley
2	medium onions, chopped		

Combine the chicken, 3 quarts water, 2 whole onions, carrots, mace and 1 teaspoon salt in a large stockpot. Bring to a boil. Boil until the chicken is tender. Cool.

Remove the chicken to a dish, reserving the stock. Chop the chicken, discarding the skin and bones. Skim and strain the reserved stock, discarding the whole onions and carrots.

Melt the butter in a large stockpot. Add 1 teaspoon salt and curry powder. Add the chopped onions, Brussels sprouts, ham and chicken. Sauté for 10 minutes. Add the tomatoes and rice and mix well. Add the reserved stock. Simmer until the rice is tender.

Blend the flour in $1/4$ cup water. Add to the stockpot. Season with white pepper. Cook until thickened, stirring constantly. Ladle into soup bowls. Top with the hard-cooked eggs and parsley.

Fiddlehead Soup

Yield: 4 servings

4	cups fresh fiddlehead ferns	2	cups milk or cream
2	tablespoons (1/4 stick) unsalted butter	1/2	teaspoon lemon zest
1	small onion, minced	•	Pepper to taste
2	cups chicken stock	•	Paprika to taste

Cook the fiddlehead ferns in boiling water in a saucepan for 6 to 8 minutes or until pale green; drain. Rinse with cold water; chop coarsely.

Melt the butter in a medium saucepan. Add the onion. Cook over medium heat until soft. Add the fiddlehead ferns and chicken stock. Bring to a gentle boil.

Cook, covered, for 5 minutes. Add the milk and reduce the heat. Bring nearly to a boil; do not boil. Season with lemon zest and pepper. Ladle into soup bowls. Sprinkle with paprika.

The highest point of coastal land between Canada and Brazil is Cadillac Mountain in Acadia National Park at 1,530 feet. Between October and May, the first rays of sunlight in the country are found here.

Casco Bay Fish Chowder

Yield: 8 to 10 servings

2	pounds haddock fillets	2	teaspoons salt
4	potatoes, peeled, chopped	1/4	teaspoon thyme
3	medium onions, chopped	1/4	teaspoon freshly ground pepper
1	garlic clove, minced	1/8	teaspoon ground cloves
1/2	cup (1 stick) butter or	1/2	cup dry white wine
	margarine, melted	2	cups boiling water
1	bay leaf	2	cups half-and-half
1	tablespoon parsley flakes		

Place the fish, potatoes, onions, garlic, melted butter and bay leaf in a large baking dish. Sprinkle with parsley flakes, salt, thyme, pepper and cloves. Add the white wine and boiling water.

Bake, covered, at 350 degrees for 1 hour. Remove the bay leaf.

Heat the half-and-half in a saucepan until scalded. Add to the chowder and stir to flake the fish.

Surfside Lentil and Pasta Soup

Yield: 8 servings

1	medium onion, finely chopped	1	carrot, finely chopped
4	garlic cloves, minced	2	ribs celery, finely chopped
1/4	cup olive oil	1	fresh tomato, chopped
1	teaspoon salt	1	(8-ounce) can tomato sauce
1/2	teaspoon black pepper	12	cups hot water
1/2	teaspoon thyme	1	pound dried lentils, sorted, rinsed
1/2	teaspoon oregano		
1	teaspoon basil	1	pound acini di pepe, cooked, drained
1/4	teaspoon crushed red pepper		
3	bay leaves		

Sauté the onion and garlic in the olive oil in an 8-quart stockpot over low heat for 5 minutes. Add the salt, black pepper, thyme, oregano, basil, red pepper, bay leaves, carrot, celery, tomato and tomato sauce.

Simmer for 5 minutes. Watch carefully to prevent burning. Add the hot water and lentils and stir to mix well. Boil slowly, covered, for 1 hour, stirring occasionally.

Remove the bay leaves. Stir in the pasta, adding additional water if needed. Serve topped with grated Romano cheese.

Lentil Soup with Tomatoes and Spinach

Yield: 8 servings

2	cups lentils, sorted, rinsed	•	Pepper to taste
6	cups water	1	pound chopped fresh spinach, or
1	large onion, quartered, sliced		1 (10-ounce) package frozen
2	garlic cloves, minced		spinach
1/4	cup olive oil	1	(28-ounce) can crushed tomatoes
1 1/2	teaspoons salt	•	Juice of 1 large lemon

Simmer the lentils in the water in a 6-quart stockpot for 1 1/2 hours. Sauté the onion and garlic in the olive oil in a skillet until tender.

Purée the lentils in the stockpot with a hand-held blender. Add the sautéed onion mixture. Season with salt and pepper. Cook for 1 hour. Add the spinach and tomatoes. Simmer for 30 minutes. Stir in the lemon juice. Serve with a paper-thin slice of lemon in each bowl.

Note: May add 1 package firm tofu, cubed, with the spinach.

Cold Lettuce Soup

Yield: 4 servings

2	heads butter lettuce	2	cups chicken stock
2	tablespoons vegetable oil	2	egg yolks
1	bunch green onions, chopped	2/3	cup half-and-half
1	garlic clove, crushed	•	Salt and pepper to taste

Rinse and trim the lettuce, discarding any damaged leaves. Reserve a few lettuce leaves for garnish. Shred the remaining lettuce leaves.

Heat the vegetable oil in a large saucepan. Add the green onions and garlic. Sauté until tender. Add the shredded lettuce. Cook, covered, until wilted. Pour in the chicken stock. Simmer for 15 minutes. Pour the soup through a sieve set over a large bowl. Return the strained soup to the saucepan.

Beat the egg yolks, half-and-half, salt and pepper in a small bowl. Stir into the soup. Simmer until thickened, stirring constantly. Do not boil. Cool. Chill in the refrigerator.

To serve, roll up the reserved lettuce leaves and cut into slices. Stir into the cold soup to garnish.

"Down East" Gazpacho

Yield: 4 servings

2	(1- to 1¹/₄-pound) lobsters, cooked	1	tablespoon snipped fresh basil
2	cups chopped peeled tomatoes	1	tablespoon olive oil
¹/₂	cup tomato juice	1	tablespoon lemon juice
¹/₄	cup finely chopped peeled cucumber	¹/₂	small garlic clove, minced
		¹/₂	teaspoon cumin (optional)
¹/₄	cup chopped green bell pepper	¹/₄	teaspoon hot pepper sauce
¹/₄	cup chopped onion	•	Pinch of celery salt
		•	Salt and pepper to taste

Remove the shells from the lobsters, keeping the shelled claws in tack. Reserve the shelled claws for serving. Chop the lobster meat.

Process the tomatoes, tomato juice, cucumber, green pepper and onion in a blender or food processor for 2 minutes. Add the basil, olive oil, lemon juice, garlic, cumin, hot pepper sauce, celery salt, salt and pepper. Blend for 30 seconds. Pour into a large bowl. Stir in the lobster meat. Chill, covered, for 2 to 24 hours.

To serve, ladle the gazpacho into large mugs. Place a reserved lobster claw in each mug.

Speedy Mushroom Soup

Yield: 6 to 8 servings

8 ounces fresh mushrooms	1 tablespoon flour
1 medium onion	1³/4 cups homemade or canned
²/3 cup fresh chopped parsley	beef broth (14 ounces)
¹/4 cup (¹/2 stick) butter	1 cup sour cream

Process the mushrooms and onion in a food processor until chopped. Add the parsley and pulse a few more times.

Melt the butter in a skillet. Add the mushroom mixture. Sauté for 5 minutes. Stir in the flour and beef broth. Bring to a boil. Cook until thickened, stirring constantly.

Process the soup and sour cream ¹/2 at a time in a food processor until blended, pouring into a saucepan after each batch. Cook the processed soup until heated through or serve chilled.

Note: May substitute zucchini for the mushrooms and yogurt for the sour cream.

The hemlock tree is found in abundance in Maine. The native Indians made tea from the leaves that contained vitamin C and thus protected them from many diseases, including scurvy.

Pasta Fagioli

Yield: 4 to 6 servings

2$^{1}/_{4}$ cups dried white beans
3 to 4 tablespoons olive oil
1 medium carrot, finely chopped
1 medium onion, finely chopped
2 ribs celery, finely chopped
5 medium garlic cloves, chopped
$^{1}/_{2}$ cup chopped fresh parsley
3 to 4 quarts homemade or canned low-sodium chicken broth

4 cups water
$^{1}/_{2}$ teaspoon oregano
• Salt and freshly ground pepper to taste
12 ounces small pasta, such as orecchiette or elbow

Rinse and sort the beans. Soak the beans in water to cover in a bowl for 8 to 12 hours; drain.

Heat the olive oil in a large saucepan. Add the carrot, onion, celery, garlic and parsley. Sauté until soft. Do not burn the garlic. Stir in the beans. Add 1 quart of the broth and 4 cups water. Bring to a boil.

Simmer for 1$^{1}/_{2}$ hours. Add the remaining broth. Season with oregano, salt and pepper. Bring to a boil. Add the pasta. Cook for 8 minutes or until the pasta is al dente. Serve hot.

Note: May substitute 3 to 4 cans cannellini beans for the white beans.

Dutch Pea Soup

Yield: 8 servings

1	pound split peas, rinsed, drained	2	cloves, crushed
3	quarts water	1	bay leaf
2	large ham hocks	6	peppercorns, crushed
4	ounces smoked bacon, chopped	1/4	teaspoon mace
3	leeks, chopped	1	rib celery with leaves, chopped
1	large onion, coarsely chopped	1	pound kielbasa or knockwurst,
2	medium carrots, coarsely		cut into 1/4-inch slices
	chopped	•	Salt and pepper to taste
1	celery root, peeled, cut	1/2	cup chopped parsley
	into halves		

Combine the peas, water, ham hocks, bacon, leeks, onion and carrots in a large stockpot. Add 1/2 of the celery root, cloves, bay leaf, peppercorns and mace. Bring to a boil and reduce the heat. Simmer, partially covered, for 2 hours or until the peas are soft, stirring occasionally.

Remove the ham hocks to a platter. Shred the ham, discarding the bones. Mince the remaining celery root. Add the ham, minced celery root and celery to the pea mixture. Simmer for 30 minutes or until the vegetables are tender, stirring occasionally. Add the kielbasa. Cook for 5 minutes. Season with salt and pepper. Sprinkle with parsley. Remove the bay leaf before serving.

Note: This soup freezes well.

Curried Pumpkin Soup

Yield: 6 to 8 servings

1/4	cup (1/2 stick) margarine	1/4	teaspoon fresh grated nutmeg
1	large onion, finely chopped	1/4	teaspoon ginger
1	leek bulb, finely chopped	1	bay leaf
1	(16-ounce) can pumpkin purée	1/2	cup half-and-half or skimmed
1	quart fat-free chicken broth		evaporated milk
1/2	teaspoon curry powder		

Melt the margarine in a 3-quart saucepan. Add the onion and leek. Sauté until soft. Stir in the pumpkin, chicken broth, curry powder, nutmeg, ginger and bay leaf. Bring to a boil and reduce the heat, stirring constantly.

Simmer, uncovered, for 15 minutes. Remove the bay leaf. Strain the solids from the liquid and place in a blender container. Process until smooth; return to the liquid in the saucepan. Add the half-and-half. Cook over medium heat until heated through, stirring constantly. Do not boil.

Squash and Apple Soup

Yield: 8 servings

1	pound butternut squash	2	to 3 broth cans water
3	tart apples	3	slices white bread, torn
1	onion, chopped	1	teaspoon salt
1/4	teaspoon rosemary	1/4	teaspoon pepper
1/4	teaspoon marjoram	1	cup light cream
3	(15-ounce) cans chicken broth		

Peel the squash and cut into quarters. Peel the apples and cut into quarters. Combine the squash, apples, onion, rosemary, marjoram, chicken broth, water, bread, salt and pepper in a large stockpot. Simmer, covered, for 45 minutes. Process in batches in a blender until smooth. Return to the stockpot. Stir in the cream just before serving. Garnish with parsley.

Wild Rice and Mushroom Soup

Yield: 6 servings

1/4	cup wild rice	1/2	cup flour
4	cups chicken stock	1/2	teaspoon salt
1/2	cup chopped celery	1/4	teaspoon white pepper
1/4	cup chopped onions	1/2	teaspoon chopped garlic
2	tablespoons sliced fresh mushrooms	2	tablespoons almonds
		1	tablespoon chopped pimento
1/2	cup chopped green bell pepper	1 1/2	cups cream
1/4	cup (1/2 stick) butter		

Cook the rice in the chicken stock in a saucepan for 30 minutes or until tender.

Sauté the celery, onions, mushrooms and green pepper in the butter in a large skillet. Add the flour. Cook for 2 minutes, stirring constantly.

Add the rice mixture, salt, white pepper, garlic, almonds and pimento and mix well. Adjust the seasonings. Stir in the cream. Cook until heated through. Do not boil. Serve immediately.

Two Lights Lobster Salad

Yield: 4 to 6 servings

1	cup wild rice	3	scallions, thinly sliced
4	cups water	1	tomato, seeded, chopped
8	ounces fresh or frozen lobster meat	1	red bell pepper, seeded, thinly sliced
2	sliced portobello mushrooms	•	Herb Dressing

Bring the rice and water to a boil in a saucepan. Cook for 30 to 45 minutes or until the water is absorbed. Fluff with a fork. Add the lobster meat, mushrooms, scallions, tomato and red pepper and toss to mix. Add the Herb Dressing and toss lightly. Spoon into a large bowl. Chill, covered, for 1 hour.

Herb Dressing

1	teaspoon sugar	2	tablespoons chopped parsley
1	teaspoon cider vinegar	2	tablespoons sherry
1	teaspoon minced garlic	2	tablespoons olive oil
1	tablespoon chives		

Dissolve the sugar in the vinegar in a bowl. Add the garlic, chives, parsley and sherry and stir until blended. Add the olive oil gradually, whisking constantly until blended.

Grilled Shrimp Caesar Salad

Yield: 4 servings

3	tablespoons lemon juice	32	jumbo shrimp, peeled, deveined
2	teaspoons anchovy paste	1/3	cup margarine
1	teaspoon bottled minced garlic	1/4	teaspoon garlic powder
1/4	teaspoon salt	8	slices French or Italian baguette
1/4	teaspoon freshly ground pepper	1	large head romaine, rinsed, torn
3/4	cup extra-virgin olive oil	2	ounces Parmesan cheese, shaved

Combine the lemon juice, anchovy paste, garlic, salt and pepper in a blender container. Add the olive oil in a fine stream, processing constantly until blended. Place 3 tablespoons of the dressing in a sealable food storage bag. Chill the remaining dressing.

Place the shrimp in the dressing in the storage bag. Seal the bag and toss until the shrimp are coated. Marinate in the refrigerator for 1 to 2 hours, tossing occasionally.

Mix the margarine and garlic powder in a microwave-safe bowl. Microwave on High until margarine is melted. Spread on the baguette slices. Place on a baking sheet. Bake at 350 degrees until toasted.

Place the shrimp in a grill basket sprayed with nonstick cooking spray. Grill for 4 minutes or until the shrimp turn pink.

Toss the romaine with the remaining dressing in a large bowl. Divide among 4 salad plates. Top each with 8 grilled shrimp and 2 baguette slices. Sprinkle with Parmesan cheese.

Asian Spinach Pork Salad

Yield: 4 servings

1	pound pork tenderloin	1	tablespoon rice vinegar
1/4	cup chopped scallions	1	tablespoon water
1	teaspoon dark sesame oil	8	cups torn spinach
2	tablespoons low-sodium soy sauce	1	(2-ounce) jar diced pimento, drained
1	tablespoon honey	2	tablespoons grated Gruyère cheese or Swiss cheese
1	teaspoon ground ginger		
1/2	teaspoon freshly ground pepper	2	tablespoons sesame seeds, toasted
1	teaspoon bottled minced garlic		
2	teaspoons dark sesame oil		

Trim the fat from the pork. Cut the pork into thin strips. Combine the scallions, 1 teaspoon sesame oil, soy sauce, honey, ginger, pepper and garlic in a sealable food storage bag. Add the pork. Seal the bag and toss to coat well.

Remove and drain the pork. Coat a broiler pan with nonstick cooking spray. Broil the pork for 4 minutes on each side or until cooked through.

Whisk 2 teaspoons sesame oil, rice vinegar and water in a bowl. Toss with the spinach in a large bowl. Divide among 4 salad plates. Top with the pork, pimento, Gruyère cheese and sesame seeds.

Note: May substitute shrimp or lean beef for the pork.

Cranberry Chicken Jellied Salad

Yield: 4 servings

1 (16-ounce) can jellied cranberry sauce
1 cup cold water
1 (3-ounce) package cranberry gelatin
• Dash of salt
3/4 cup drained pineapple

1 envelope unflavored gelatin
1 cup cold water
1 cup mayonnaise
1/2 cup evaporated milk
1/2 teaspoon salt
3/4 cup chopped celery
2 cups chopped cooked chicken

Mash the cranberry sauce in 1 cup cold water in a saucepan. Bring to a boil. Add the cranberry gelatin.

Heat until smooth and the cranberry gelatin dissolves, stirring frequently. Season with a dash of salt. Chill until partially set. Fold in the pineapple. Pour into a lightly oiled 3-quart glass dish.

Soften the unflavored gelatin in 1 cup cold water in a double boiler. Heat over hot water until the gelatin dissolves, stirring frequently. Add the mayonnaise, evaporated milk, 1/2 teaspoon salt and celery. Pour over the cranberry layer. Sprinkle with the chicken. Chill until set.

Sundance Black Bean and Corn Salad

Yield: 4 to 6 servings

Great served for summer picnics and cookouts.

1   (16-ounce) can small black beans, drained

1   (16-ounce) can whole kernel corn, drained

1   cup cherry tomato halves

1   cup chopped green, red and/or yellow bell pepper

1   red onion, chopped

1/4   cup chopped fresh parsley

•   Italian salad dressing or vinaigrette to taste

1   cup Havarti cheese cubes

•   Blue and yellow corn chips

Combine the black beans, corn, tomatoes, bell pepper, red onion and parsley in a large bowl. Add the salad dressing and toss to mix well. Chill, covered, until ready to serve.

To serve, add the cheese and toss gently. Spoon in the middle of a large round platter. Surround the salad with blue and yellow corn chips.

Cannellini Bean Salad

Yield: 4 to 6 servings

Excellent low-cholesterol dish.

1	head lettuce, torn	•	Juice of 1 lemon
1/2	red bell pepper, finely chopped	3	tablespoons olive oil
1/2	green bell pepper, finely chopped	1	tablespoon vinegar
1/2	cup chopped fresh parsley	1/4	teaspoon oregano
1	(20-ounce) can cannellini beans, drained	1/4	teaspoon tarragon
1	(20-ounce) can chick-peas, drained	1	teaspoon dried basil

Combine the lettuce, red pepper, green pepper, parsley, beans, chick-peas, lemon juice, olive oil and vinegar in a large bowl and toss to mix well. Sprinkle with the oregano, tarragon and basil and toss gently.

Joan Benoit Samuelson, the great distance runner, was born in Cape Elizabeth, Maine. In both 1979 and 1982 she won the women's division of the Boston Marathon.

Greek Bean and Tomato Salad

Yield: 4 to 6 servings

2	cups snapped fresh green beans	1/4	cup chopped green onions
1	cup bite-size fresh red tomato pieces	•	Fresh chopped dill to taste
1/2	cup crumbled feta cheese	•	Dill Vinaigrette

Parboil the green beans in water to cover in a saucepan for 3 to 4 minutes or until tender-crisp. Drain immediately and chill in the refrigerator.

Combine the chilled green beans and tomatoes in a bowl. Add the feta cheese, green onions and dill and toss gently. Add the Dill Vinaigrette and toss to coat. Serve at room temperature or chill until ready to serve.

Dill Vinaigrette

1/2	cup olive oil	1	teaspoon oregano
5	tablespoons red wine vinegar	1/2	teaspoon salt
1	garlic clove, crushed	1/4	teaspoon freshly ground pepper
1/4	cup snipped fresh dill, or 1 1/2 tablespoons dried dill		

Combine the olive oil, red wine vinegar, garlic, dill, oregano, salt and pepper in a jar with a tight-fitting lid. Cover and shake well.

Captain's Caesar Salad

Yield: 5 to 6 servings

1/4	cup olive oil	4	drops of Worcestershire sauce
3	small garlic cloves, or 2 large garlic cloves	•	Salt and pepper to taste
2	eggs	1	large head romaine, rinsed, chilled, torn
•	Juice of 1/2 lemon	•	Grated Parmesan cheese to taste
1 1/2	tablespoons vinegar	•	Restaurant-style croutons to taste

Process the olive oil, garlic, eggs, lemon juice, vinegar, Worcestershire sauce, salt and pepper in a blender at high speed until blended.

Toss the romaine with the dressing in a large salad bowl. Add the Parmesan cheese and toss gently. Sprinkle with croutons.

Editor's Note: In order to avoid the risk of salmonella from the use of raw egg yolk, follow this method of allowing the egg yolk to reach a temperature of 200 degrees without fully cooking it. Mix 1 egg yolk with 1 tablespoon lemon juice or vinegar and 1 tablespoon water in a small glass bowl. Whisk until well combined. Cover the bowl. Microwave on High for 30 seconds or until the mixture begins to rise. Microwave for 5 seconds longer. Beat again with a clean wire whisk until smooth. Microwave on High for 10 seconds or until the mixture rises again. Beat again with a clean wire whisk until smooth. The mixture should be at 200 degrees. Cover the bowl and let stand for 1 minute before using.

Orzo Feta Salad

Yield: 8 servings

Delicious served for lunch on a summer day.

4	cups cooked orzo, at room temperature	3	tablespoons chopped fresh chives
3	cups chopped cucumbers	2	tablespoons olive oil
1	cup crumbled feta cheese	2	tablespoons balsamic vinegar
1/2	cup chopped red onion	2	tablespoons lemon juice
		1/4	teaspoon pepper

Combine the orzo, cucumbers, feta cheese, red onion and chives in a large bowl and toss gently. Combine the olive oil, balsamic vinegar, lemon juice and pepper in a small bowl and blend well. Add to the orzo mixture and mix well. Chill in the refrigerator.

Chafing Dish Spinach Salad

Yield: 4 to 6 servings

1	pound fresh spinach	1	teaspoon sugar
4	or 5 green onions, sliced	1/2	teaspoon salt
•	Freshly ground pepper to taste	1	hard-cooked egg, coarsely chopped
5	slices bacon, chopped	•	Sliced mushrooms to taste
2	tablespoons wine vinegar		
1	tablespoon lemon juice		

Rinse the spinach, discarding the stems; pat dry. Tear the spinach into bite-size pieces and place in a large bowl. Add the green onions. Sprinkle with pepper. Chill in the refrigerator.

Fry the bacon in a chafing dish or large skillet until crisp. Add the wine vinegar, lemon juice, sugar and salt and mix well. Add the spinach and toss until coated and slightly wilted. Place on serving plates. Sprinkle with chopped hard-cooked eggs and sliced mushrooms. Serve immediately.

Watercress and Pear Salad

Yield: 4 to 6 servings

2	bunches watercress		1/3	cup balsamic vinegar
2	firm red pears, thinly sliced		1	teaspoon sugar
1/2 to 3/4	cup pecan halves, toasted		1/2	teaspoon salt
1/2 to 3/4	cup crumbled feta cheese		1/4	teaspoon freshly ground pepper
1/2	cup chopped green onions		2/3	cup olive oil

Rinse the watercress, discarding the stems. Tear the watercress into bite-size pieces and place in a large salad bowl. Arrange the pears over the watercress. Sprinkle with pecans, feta cheese and green onions.

Combine the balsamic vinegar, sugar, salt, pepper and olive oil in a jar with a tight-fitting lid. Cover and shake until mixed. Drizzle over the watercress salad. Serve immediately.

Note: May substitute apples for the pears and bleu cheese for the feta cheese. May add dried cranberries and red, yellow or orange bell pepper.

Accompaniments
Vegetables and Sides

Accompaniments
Vegetables and Sides

Boston Baked Beans

Yield: 6 to 8 servings

2	cups dried pea beans	1	tablespoon sugar
4	ounces salt pork, scalded, scraped	1	teaspoon salt
1/2	cup molasses	1/2	teaspoon prepared mustard

Soak the beans in water to cover in a bowl for 8 to 12 hours; drain. Place the beans in a large saucepan. Add enough water to cover. Cook over low heat until the skins burst. Drain, reserving the cooking liquid.

Place a 1/4-inch slice of the salt pork in the bottom of a 2-quart bean pot. Add the beans. Bury the remaining salt pork in the beans.

Bring the reserved cooking liquid to a boil in a saucepan. Add 1 cup of the boiling liquid to the molasses, sugar, salt and mustard in a bowl and mix well. Pour over the beans in the bean pot. Add enough of the remaining cooking liquid to just cover the beans.

Bake, covered, at 225 degrees for 6 to 8 hours, adding additional water as needed and uncovering for the last hour of baking.

English Walnut Broccoli

Yield: 8 servings

2	(10-ounce) packages frozen broccoli	2	cups milk
•	Salt to taste	6	tablespoons ($^3/_4$ stick) butter
$^1/_2$	cup (1 stick) butter	$^2/_3$	cup water
$^1/_4$	cup flour	$^2/_3$	(16-ounce) package herb stuffing mix
4	chicken bouillon cubes, crushed	$^2/_3$	cup chopped English walnuts

Cook the broccoli in boiling salted water to cover in a saucepan until tender; drain. Place in a greased 2-quart baking dish.

Melt $^1/_2$ cup butter in a saucepan. Blend in the flour and bouillon cubes to form a paste. Add the milk gradually, stirring constantly. Cook until thickened and smooth, stirring constantly. Pour over the broccoli.

Melt 6 tablespoons butter in $^2/_3$ cup water in a saucepan. Pour over the stuffing mix in a bowl and toss to coat. Stir in the walnuts. Spoon over the top of the sauce. Bake at 350 degrees for 30 minutes.

Don't Believe It's Broccoli

Yield: 8 to 10 servings

Adapted from a fried appetizer served in a Boston restaurant, this recipe could even command a "Presidential" seal of approval by George.

2 sleeves butter crackers (8 ounces)
1/2 cup grated Parmesan cheese
3/4 cup mayonnaise
1 large bunch broccoli, cut into spears

2 cups shredded Cheddar cheese
1 cup shredded mozzarella cheese
• Sour cream

Process the crackers in a food processor fitted with a steel blade until finely crushed or place in a plastic food bag and crush with a rolling pin.

Mix the cracker crumbs, Parmesan cheese and mayonnaise in a bowl until the mixture resembles coarse meal.

Steam the broccoli in a steamer until tender-crisp; do not overcook.

Arrange the broccoli in a single layer in a buttered 9x13-inch baking dish, alternating the spears. Layer the Cheddar cheese, cracker mixture and mozzarella cheese evenly over the broccoli. Bake at 325 degrees for 25 to 30 minutes or until the top layer is golden brown. Serve with sour cream.

Pan-Seared Cabbage Slaw

Yield: 6 to 8 servings

Serve with roasted meats, corned beef and chicken. Incorporate into a southern menu and serve with barbecue and corn bread. Mix with home-fried potatoes and kielbasa sausage for a great skillet dish.

1	large head green cabbage		1	teaspoon celery seeds
1/4	cup canola or vegetable oil		1	tablespoon instant beef bouillon
1	pound carrots, shredded		•	Coarsely ground pepper to taste

Cut the cabbage into halves and remove the core. Place each half cut side down on a cutting board. Cut each into thin strips.

Heat a Dutch oven over medium-high heat. Add the canola oil. Add the cabbage and carrots. Cook until the cabbage begins to render some liquid, tossing constantly with a wooden spoon. Reduce the heat only if the cabbage begins to burn. Continue cooking until the vegetables are reduced by 1/2. Add the celery seeds, instant bouillon and pepper. Cook until of the desired consistency.

Note: The longer the vegetables cook, the more tender and sweet they will become.

Carrot and Turnip Purée

Yield: 4 to 6 servings

The bright orange color and smooth texture makes this
dish welcomed even by children.

1   (3-pound) turnip, cut into
    1-inch pieces
3   pounds carrots, cut into
    1-inch pieces

- Butter to taste
- Salt and pepper to taste

Place the turnip and carrots in separate saucepans and add enough cold water to each to cover. Bring each to a boil. Boil until tender when pierced with a fork. Pour each into separate colanders to drain. Let stand for a few minutes until all of the liquid has drained out of each colander.

Process the turnip and carrots a small amount at a time with a few pats of butter in a food processor until smooth, pouring into a large bowl after each batch. Season with salt and pepper to taste. Spoon into a serving dish and keep warm or reheat.

Note: This recipe only requires an equal weight of turnips to carrots. It is best made several days in advance and can be reheated in a microwave or in a baking dish along side the turkey or other meat while roasting.

Creamy Colorful Cauliflower

Yield: 12 servings

Serve this flavorful vegetable combination with grilled fish or meat.

1	large head cauliflower	3	to 4 ribs celery, sliced
1	large bunch broccoli	1	large red bell pepper, seeded,
1	pound baby carrots, sliced		sliced
1	(16-ounce) package frozen	•	Dijon Dressing
	green peas		

Cut the cauliflower and broccoli into bite-size pieces, discarding the stems.

Steam the cauliflower, broccoli and carrots separately in a steamer until tender-crisp. Do not overcook. Plunge each immediately into a bowl of ice water to stop the cooking process, placing the green peas in the water before the last vegetable is added and adding more ice as needed.

Place the vegetables in a large colander. Let stand for a few minutes until all the excess water has drained from the vegetables. Place the drained vegetables in a large bowl. Add the celery and red pepper. Add the Dijon Dressing and toss gently to coat. Chill, covered, for 6 to 12 hours.

Dijon Dressing

1	cup mayonnaise	2	teaspoons celery seeds
1/2	cup Dijon or spicy brown	1/2	cup chopped fresh chives, or
	mustard		1/4 cup frozen dried chives
1	cup sour cream	•	Salt and pepper to taste
2	tablespoons tarragon		

Combine the mayonnaise, Dijon mustard and sour cream in a bowl and mix well. Stir in the tarragon, celery seeds, chives, salt and pepper to taste.

Katahdin Corn Pudding

Yield: 4 servings

Prepare this easy dish for potluck suppers.

6	ears of fresh corn	2	teaspoons sugar
2	eggs	1	teaspoon salt
2	tablespoons (1/4 stick) butter, melted	•	Dash of pepper

Shuck the corn and discard the silks. Cut the kernels from the cobs into a bowl, scraping the cobs to extract the milk; discard the cobs.

Add the eggs, butter, sugar, salt and pepper and mix well. Pour into a greased 9x9-inch baking dish with 1 1/2-inch sides. Bake at 350 degrees for 1 hour.

Note: This recipe can be doubled.

L.L. Bean is one of the country's most notable retail stores and is a testament to Maine's commitment to preserving the outdoor experience. It was founded by Leon Leonwood Bean, an industrious Mainer, who built his retailing empire through hard work and a determination to satisfy his customers. After coming back from hunting with wet, sore feet, he went to a local cobbler and had him cut the bottoms from a pair of rubber boots and attach them to the upper parts of a pair of leather boots. He then made some for his friends and sold some more to other hunters, but never considered the sale complete until the customer was satisfied. Today the famous "Bean Boot" is sold around the world.

Ocean Onion Bake

Yield: variable

- Summer onion bulbs
- Slivered garlic
- Chopped Gruyère cheese
- Grated Parmesan cheese
- Coarsely ground pepper
- Pinch of thyme
- Heavy cream
- Paprika to taste
- Butter to taste

Place an onion per serving snuggly in a buttered baking dish. Sprinkle with garlic, Gruyère cheese, Parmesan cheese, pepper and thyme. Pour enough cream into the dish to come 3/4 up the side of the onions.

Bake at 300 to 325 degrees for 1 hour or until the onions absorb the cream and are golden brown. Sprinkle with paprika and dot with butter before serving.

*The start of the Appalachian Trail is in Maine on Mount Katahdin, which is
5,267 feet high. It was revered by Maine Indians as the abode of their great hero-god Glooskap.
It became a state park in 1931 when Percival Baxter, using his personal fortune, bought it
from the Great Northern Paper Company and gave it as a gift to the people of Maine.*

Baked Vidalia Onions

Yield: 4 to 6 servings

Delicious served with burgers, chicken or seafood during the cookout season.

4	large Vidalia onions	$^2/_3$	cup chicken or beef broth
$^1/_4$	cup ($^1/_2$ stick) butter	$^1/_3$	cup dry sherry
2	tablespoons flour	•	Fresh bread crumbs

Peel the onions and slice $^1/_2$ inch thick. Sauté the onions in the butter in a skillet until translucent. Stir in the flour. Add the broth and sherry. Spoon into a buttered small baking dish. Cover the top with bread crumbs.

Bake at 325 degrees for 20 to 25 minutes or until bubbly and brown on top.

Note: May decrease the butter to 2 tablespoons ($^1/_4$ stick) and add 2 tablespoons olive oil. May also freeze before baking. Thaw and bake when ready to serve to extend the Vidalia onion season.

Holiday Mashed Potatoes

Yield: 8 to 12 servings

12	medium potatoes, peeled	1/2	cup milk
8	ounces cream cheese, softened	2	eggs, lightly beaten
1/2	cup (1 stick) butter	•	Salt and pepper to taste
1/2	cup sour cream		

Boil the potatoes in water to cover in a saucepan until tender; drain. Mash the potatoes. Add the cream cheese and butter and beat until smooth. Add the sour cream and mix well.

Mix the milk and eggs in a bowl. Add to the potato mixture with salt and pepper and beat until light and fluffy. Spoon into a greased 2-quart baking dish. Chill, covered, for 8 to 12 hours. Bake, uncovered, at 350 degrees for 45 minutes.

Nearly 80 percent of the lobster harvest is caught between July and November.
Each lobsterman will haul as many as several hundred traps per day.

Lobster and Potato Cakes

Yield: 4 to 6 servings

8	ounces fresh or frozen lobster meat, chopped		2	teaspoons finely chopped chives
2	cups mashed cooked potatoes		2	tablespoons vegetable oil
1	tablespoon dry mustard		1/3	cup sour cream
1 1/2	teaspoons fresh lemon juice		•	Sprigs of fresh dillweed
2	teaspoons finely chopped dillweed			

Combine the lobster meat and mashed potatoes in a bowl and mix well. Add the dry mustard, lemon juice, dillweed and chives and stir until blended. Shape into 2-inch balls and flatten into patties.

Heat a medium skillet. Add the vegetable oil. Add the patties to the hot oil. Cook until golden brown, turning once. Top each with a dollop of sour cream and a sprig of fresh dillweed. Serve immediately.

Taste-of-the-Islands Taters

Yield: 6 to 8 servings

These untraditional sweet potatoes make a great side dish for any tropical menu.

3   to 4 pounds sweet potatoes or yams
4   ounces dark rum
1   cup (2 sticks) butter
4   ounces cream of coconut (optional)

- Pinch of nutmeg
- Pinch of cinnamon
- Salt and pepper to taste

Peel the sweet potatoes and cut into small pieces. Bring to a boil in cold water to cover in a saucepan. Cook until tender when pierced with a fork. Pour into a colander to drain. Let stand for a few minutes to remove any excess water.

Place the sweet potatoes in a large mixer bowl. Pour the rum over the hot sweet potatoes and add the butter.

Beat at low speed until combined. Beat at high speed until smooth. Add the cream of coconut, nutmeg and cinnamon and beat well. Season with salt and pepper. Spoon into a serving bowl and serve immediately.

Vegetable Mumbo Stew

Yield: 6 to 8 servings

This side dish is a low-cholesterol treat.

2	medium onions, coarsely chopped
4	to 6 garlic cloves, chopped
1/4	cup olive oil
4	carrots, coarsely chopped
6	to 8 fresh tomatoes, coarsely chopped
2	to 4 zucchini, coarsely chopped
2	(28-ounce) cans peeled plum tomatoes
1	(6-ounce) can tomato paste
1	bunch fresh dill, chopped
1	bunch fresh Italian parsley, chopped
1	cup chopped fresh basil
1	teaspoon oregano
•	Salt and freshly ground pepper to taste

Sauté the onions and garlic in olive oil in a 5- to 7-quart saucepan. Add the carrots, tomatoes, zucchini, plum tomatoes, tomato paste, dill, Italian parsley, basil, oregano, salt and pepper and mix well. Bring to a boil and reduce the heat. Simmer for 1 to 2 hours or until of the desired consistency, stirring occasionally.

Note: May substitute 1 large eggplant for the zucchini.

Barley and Pine Nut Pilaf

Yield: 6 servings

Excellent served with poultry or lamb.

1	cup pearl barley	$1/2$	cup chopped fresh parsley
6	tablespoons ($3/4$ stick) butter or margarine	$1/4$	teaspoon salt
$1/3$	cup pine nuts	$1/4$	teaspoon pepper
1	cup chopped green onions	$3^1/3$	cups chicken broth

Rinse the barley in cold water and drain. Melt the butter in a 10-inch skillet. Add the pine nuts. Sauté until the pine nuts are brown. Remove the pine nuts from the skillet with a slotted spoon and reserve.

Sauté the green onions and barley in the skillet until lightly toasted. Remove from the heat. Stir in the reserved pine nuts, parsley, salt and pepper. Spoon into an ungreased 2-quart baking dish.

Bring the chicken broth to a boil in a saucepan. Pour over the barley mixture and stir to mix well. Bake, uncovered, at 350 degrees for 1 hour and 10 minutes.

Parmesan Polenta

Yield: 4 servings

This is a great alternative to rice and potatoes.

4 cups chicken stock, or canned low-salt low-fat chicken broth	1/2 cup grated Parmesan cheese
1 cup yellow cornmeal	1 1/2 tablespoons butter
	• Salt and pepper to taste

Bring the chicken stock to a boil in a large heavy saucepan. Reduce the heat to medium. Add the cornmeal gradually, whisking constantly. Cook for 5 to 10 minutes or until the mixture is thick and creamy, whisking constantly. Remove from the heat.

Stir in the Parmesan cheese and butter. Season with salt and pepper. Spoon into a serving bowl and serve immediately.

Richmond Island Rice Pilaf

Yield: 4 to 6 servings

1/4 cup (1/2 stick) butter	1 (14-ounce) can beef broth
1 cup crushed egg noodles	1 beef bouillon cube
1 (14-ounce) can chicken broth	1 cup uncooked rice

Melt the butter in a skillet. Add the crushed egg noodles. Sauté until golden brown.

Bring the chicken broth, beef broth and bouillon cube to a boil in a saucepan. Add the sautéed egg noodles and rice. Return to a boil. Reduce the heat. Simmer for 20 minutes.

Lemon Dill Rice

Yield: 8 servings

1	cup uncooked rice	2	tablespoons (¹/4 stick) margarine
3	tablespoons olive oil	¹/2	tablespoon dry dill, or ¹/4 cup
1	cup finely chopped celery		minced fresh dill
1	cup finely chopped onion	1	tablespoon sugar
1	large garlic clove, minced	•	Salt and pepper to taste
1³/4	cups chicken broth	5	lemon slices
2	tablespoons fresh lemon juice		

Sauté the rice in the olive oil in a skillet over medium heat for 5 minutes or until light brown. Add the celery and onion. Sauté for 5 minutes. Add the garlic. Sauté for 1 minute.

Add the chicken broth, lemon juice, margarine, dill, sugar, salt and pepper and mix well. Arrange the lemon slices over the top. Bring to a boil and reduce the heat.

Simmer, covered, for 18 to 20 minutes or until the rice is tender and the liquid is absorbed. Remove from the heat. Let stand, covered, for 10 minutes. Garnish with dill sprigs.

Crescendo

Brunch and Breads

Crescendo

Brunch and Breads

Curried Sausage Casserole

Yield: 6 to 8 servings

Since this recipe can be prepared in advance, it is perfect for serving to overnight guests, along with your favorite strata or egg recipe.

1	pound mild bulk pork sausage	1¹/₂ cups milk	
1	pound hot bulk pork sausage	2	teaspoons curry powder
1	medium green bell pepper, sliced	•	Salt and pepper to taste
1	cup sliced fresh mushrooms	6	ounces seasoned bread crumbs
2	tablespoons (¹/4 stick) butter	3	ounces freshly grated Parmesan
2	tablespoons flour		cheese

Brown the mild and hot sausage in a skillet, stirring until crumbly; drain. Add the green pepper and mushrooms. Cook until the vegetables are tender, stirring frequently.

Melt the butter in a heavy saucepan. Stir in the flour to make a roux. Add the milk, curry powder, salt and pepper gradually and mix well. Cook over low heat until thickened, stirring constantly. Stir in the sausage mixture. Spoon into a 9x9-inch baking dish. Sprinkle with a mixture of the bread crumbs and Parmesan cheese. Bake at 350 degrees for 30 minutes.

Note: May be prepared ahead, refrigerated or frozen, and baked as needed.

Baked Asparagus and Eggs Sunny-Side Up

Yield: 4 servings

1/4 cup (1/2 stick) butter	8 eggs
8 asparagus spears, cut into bite-size pieces	1/4 cup grated Parmesan cheese
6 slices prosciutto, cut into bite-size pieces	

Melt the butter in a skillet over medium-high heat. Add the asparagus. Cook for 2 minutes, stirring frequently.

Place the prosciutto in a greased 9x13-inch baking dish. Break the eggs carefully over the prosciutto. Pour the asparagus mixture evenly over the eggs. Sprinkle with the Parmesan cheese.

Bake at 400 degrees for 5 to 7 minutes or until the eggs are cooked through.

The National Geographic Society has placed a stone on Route 1 near Perry, Maine, to delineate the midpoint between the north pole and the equator.

Individual Egg Puffs

Yield: 10 servings

This recipe is an adaptation of a brunch recipe served at
bed-and-breakfasts in the Southwest.

10	eggs	1/2	cup (1 stick) butter, softened
3/4	cup flour	1	pound Monterey Jack cheese,
1/2	teaspoon salt		shredded
1	teaspoon baking powder	•	Freshly ground pepper to taste
16	ounces cottage cheese	1	(8-ounce) can green chiles

Beat the eggs in a mixer bowl until light and pale yellow. Add the flour, salt and baking powder, beating constantly. Mix in the cottage cheese. Add the butter, Monterey Jack cheese and pepper and mix well. Stir in the green chiles. Chill, covered, for 8 to 12 hours.

Spoon into 10 small ramekins or soufflé cups sprayed with nonstick cooking spray. Bake at 350 degrees for 30 minutes or until light brown around the edges and puffed in the center.

Coastal Quiche

Yield: 6 to 8 servings

1	recipe (1-crust) pie pastry	1	cup light cream
5	ounces Swiss cheese, shredded	1	cup whole or low-fat milk
5	ounces sharp Cheddar cheese, shredded	•	Salt and pepper to taste
•	Quiche Filling of choice	$1/8$	teaspoon garlic powder
6	eggs, beaten	$1/8$	teaspoon nutmeg

Line a 9-inch pie plate or quiche dish with the pie pastry, fluting the edge.

Sprinkle the Swiss cheese and Cheddar cheese evenly over the bottom of the pie pastry. Add the desired Quiche Filling.

Whisk the eggs, light cream, milk, salt, pepper, garlic powder and nutmeg in a bowl until blended. Pour over the Quiche Filling.

Bake at 425 degrees for 15 minutes. Reduce the oven temperature to 325 degrees. Bake for 1 hour longer or until a sharp knife inserted near the center comes out clean.

Quiche Fillings

The secret to a rich and flavorful quiche is to cook all vegetables and other filling ingredients first. Try some of the suggested fillings below, or create your own favorites.

TRADITIONAL LORRAINE

1 pound bacon, crisp-fried, crumbled

SIMPLY ELEGANT

8 ounces fresh crab meat, flaked   1 pound asparagus, steamed,

SINFUL SEAFOOD

8 ounces fresh crab meat, flaked   8 ounces sea scallops, poached,
8 ounces small shrimp, poached or   sliced
   sautéed

BASIC BROCCOLI

1 medium onion, chopped   2 cups finely chopped broccoli,
1 tablespoon butter   steamed

Sauté the onion in the butter in a skillet until tender. Combine the onion and broccoli in a bowl and mix well.

VEGETARIAN

4 cups packed spinach   2 tablespoons (¹/₄ stick) butter
1 medium onion, chopped   2 or 3 carrots, peeled, shredded
1 medium green bell pepper,   8 ounces mushrooms, chopped
   chopped

Rinse the spinach and pat dry. Remove the stems and chop the spinach. Sauté the onion and green pepper in the butter in a skillet until tender. Add the carrots. Cook until tender, stirring frequently. Add the mushrooms. Cook until tender, stirring frequently. Stir in the spinach. Cook until the liquid has been absorbed.

Crab Meat Quiches

Yield: 5 to 10 servings

Serve with a fresh spinach or fruit salad.

$^1/_2$ cup mayonnaise
2 eggs
$^1/_2$ cup milk
8 ounces fresh crab meat, flaked

8 ounces Swiss cheese, shredded
$^1/_2$ cup chopped onion
• Dash of pepper
2 unbaked (10-inch) pie shells

Process the mayonnaise, eggs, milk and crab meat in a blender until blended. Combine the egg mixture, Swiss cheese, onion and pepper in a bowl and mix well. Pour into the pie shells. Bake at 350 degrees for 40 to 45 minutes or until set.

Note: For best results, cover and freeze the unbaked quiches. Thaw at room temperature for 1 hour. Bake, covered, at 350 degrees for 45 minutes or until set.

Harriet Beecher Stowe's great contribution to American literature, Uncle Tom's Cabin,
*was written in her home on Federal Street in Brunswick. Her husband, Calvin E. Stowe,
was a professor of biblical literature at Bowdoin College in 1851.*

Lobster Quiche

Yield: 4 to 6 servings

Serve for Christmas brunch.

6	eggs, beaten	1	cup shredded Swiss cheese
1¹/₂	cups sour cream	¹/₂	cup chopped scallions
¹/₂	teaspoon Worcestershire sauce	8	ounces lobster meat, flaked
•	Freshly ground pepper to taste	1	unbaked (10-inch) pie shell
1	teaspoon Dijon mustard	•	Paprika to taste
1	cup shredded sharp Cheddar cheese		

Beat the eggs, sour cream, Worcestershire sauce, pepper and Dijon mustard in a bowl until smooth and creamy.

Combine the Cheddar cheese, Swiss cheese and scallions in a bowl and toss to mix. Stir in the lobster gently.

Place the lobster mixture in the pie shell. Pour the egg mixture over the top. Sprinkle with paprika. Bake at 375 degrees for 45 minutes or until set and puffed in the middle. Serve immediately.

Note: May cool and chill, covered, until ready to serve. To reheat, bake, uncovered, at 425 degrees for 12 minutes.

Baked Bananas

Yield: 4 servings

6	bananas, cut into $^1/_2$-inch slices	$^1/_2$	cup (1 stick) butter or margarine, melted
$^3/_4$	cup packed brown sugar	1	cup sour cream

Arrange the bananas in a 9-inch pie plate. Sprinkle the brown sugar evenly over the bananas. Drizzle the butter evenly over the brown sugar.

Bake at 375 degrees for 10 minutes. Stir gently with a wooden spoon. Bake for 10 to 20 minutes longer or until bubbly. Let stand to cool slightly. Spoon into dessert bowls. Top with dollops of sour cream.

Note: May substitute 3 cups fresh or frozen blueberries for the bananas and/or use yogurt instead of sour cream.

Brunch Oatmeal Pie

Yield: 6 to 8 servings

1	baked (10-inch) pie shell	1	tablespoon butter, melted, cooled
$1^1/_2$	cups maple syrup	1	teaspoon cinnamon
1	cup quick-cooking oats	$^1/_4$	teaspoon ground cloves
$^3/_4$	cup sugar		
4	large eggs		

Chill the pie shell while preparing the filling. Combine the maple syrup, oats, sugar, eggs, butter, cinnamon and cloves in a bowl. Whisk until well mixed. Spoon the filling into the pie shell. Bake at 400 degrees for 50 to 60 minutes or until set. Cool on a wire rack. Serve at room temperature.

Harvest Pumpkin Roll

Yield: 8 to 12 servings

3	eggs	1	teaspoon salt
1	cup sugar	1/2	teaspoon cinnamon
2/3	cup canned pumpkin	1/2	cup chopped walnuts
3/4	cup flour	•	Confectioners' sugar
1	teaspoon baking soda	•	Cream Cheese Filling

Beat the eggs in a mixer bowl until fluffy. Add the sugar gradually, beating constantly. Add the pumpkin, flour, baking soda, salt and cinnamon and mix well. Spread over a greased and waxed paper-lined baking sheet. Sprinkle with walnuts.

Bake at 375 degrees for 15 minutes. Invert onto a towel sprinkled with confectioners' sugar. Roll up into a log. Let stand until cool.

Unroll the log and remove the waxed paper. Spread with the Cream Cheese Filling and roll up. Chill, covered, until serving time. Sprinkle with additional confectioners' sugar just before serving.

Cream Cheese Filling

8	ounces cream cheese, softened	1	teaspoon vanilla extract
2	tablespoons (1/4 stick) butter, softened	1	cup confectioners' sugar

Beat the cream cheese and butter in a mixer bowl until light and fluffy. Add the vanilla and confectioners' sugar and beat until smooth.

Sweet Breakfast Babka

Yield: 24 servings

1/2	cup lukewarm water	3	eggs
2	tablespoons dry yeast	1/2	cup sugar
1	teaspoon sugar	5	cups (about) flour
2	tablespoons flour	1	teaspoon salt
1 1/2	cups milk	•	Raisins (optional)
1/2	cup (1 stick) butter, melted		

Mix the water, yeast, 1 teaspoon sugar and 2 tablespoons flour in a small bowl. Cover with a towel. Let stand for 5 to 10 minutes or until doubled in volume and foamy.

Heat the milk in a saucepan until scalded. Add the melted butter. Cool slightly.

Beat the eggs and 1/2 cup sugar in a large mixer bowl until well mixed. Add the milk mixture and mix well. Add 2 cups of the flour and salt and beat until smooth. Add the yeast mixture and mix well. Add the raisins and mix well. Stir in enough of the remaining flour to form a soft dough.

Knead the dough on a lightly floured surface until smooth and elastic. Place in a greased bowl, turning to coat the surface. Let rise for 30 to 60 minutes or until doubled in bulk. Punch the dough down and knead lightly. Divide into 2 equal portions. Shape each portion into a loaf. Place in greased 5x9-inch loaf pans. Let rise until doubled in bulk.

Place in a preheated 350-degree oven. Reduce oven temperature to 300 degrees. Bake for 45 minutes or until the loaves test done.

Cinnamon Swirl Coffee Cake

Yield: 16 servings

1/2 cup (or more) chopped walnuts	1/2 cup (1 stick) butter or margarine, melted
1/3 cup (scant) sugar	3/4 cup sugar
1 teaspoon cinnamon	1 teaspoon vanilla extract
2 cups flour	2 eggs
1 teaspoon baking powder	1 cup sour cream
1 teaspoon baking soda	
1/4 teaspoon salt	

Mix the walnuts, 1/3 cup sugar and cinnamon in a bowl. Sift the flour, baking powder, baking soda and salt together.

Combine the butter, 3/4 cup sugar and vanilla in a mixer bowl and beat well. Add the eggs 1 at a time, beating well after each addition. Add the flour mixture and mix well. Stir in the sour cream.

Layer the batter and walnut mixture 1/2 at a time in a greased tube pan. Bake at 350 degrees for 40 to 50 minutes or until the coffee cake tests done.

Banana Apple Coffee Cake

Yield: 18 to 20 servings

Due to unexpected guests, these ordinary ingredients were combined
to produce a new family favorite for breakfast or coffee time.

2 bananas, sliced	2 tablespoons flour
2 eggs	1/4 cup packed brown sugar
1 cup buttermilk	2 tablespoons (1/4 stick) margarine
1 package banana bread mix	1 large apple, peeled, sliced
1/4 cup rolled oats	

Process the bananas, eggs and buttermilk in a food processor until smooth. Combine with the banana bread mix in a bowl and stir just until moistened. Pour into a lightly greased 9x13-inch baking pan. Mix the oats, flour and brown sugar in a bowl. Cut in the margarine until crumbly. Arrange the sliced apples over the batter. Sprinkle with the oat mixture.

Bake at 350 degrees for 35 to 45 minutes or until coffee cake tests done and the top is almost dry.

Cranberry Orange Scones

Yield: 8 servings

2	cups flour	2/3	cup dried cranberries
1/3	cup sugar	•	Grated peel of 1 orange
1 1/2	teaspoons baking powder	1/2	cup plain yogurt
1/2	teaspoon baking soda	1/4	cup orange juice
1/4	teaspoon salt	1	large egg, or 2 egg whites
3	tablespoons butter or margarine		

Mix the flour, sugar, baking powder, baking soda and salt in a bowl. Cut in the butter until crumbly. Stir in the dried cranberries and orange peel.

Mix the yogurt and orange juice in a bowl. Add the egg and beat well. Add to the flour mixture and stir just until blended. Knead 3 or 4 times on a lightly floured surface. Pat into an 8-inch circle. Cut into 8 equal wedges using a serrated knife. Place the wedges on an ungreased baking sheet. Bake at 400 degrees for 12 to 15 minutes or until light brown. Serve with tea.

Agriculture in Maine generates more than $400 million a year. The greatest percentage comes from egg production. Approximately two billion potatoes are harvested annually.

Wild Maine Blueberry Muffins

Yield: 12 servings

1/2 cup (1 stick) butter or margarine, softened
1 cup sugar
2 eggs
2 cups flour
2 teaspoons baking powder
1/2 teaspoon salt
1/2 cup milk
2 cups fresh or thawed frozen Maine blueberries
• Sugar

Beat the butter and 1 cup sugar in a mixer bowl until light and fluffy. Add the eggs 1 at a time, beating well after each addition. Combine the flour, baking powder and salt and mix well. Add the flour mixture and milk alternately to the butter mixture, beating well after each addition. Fold in the blueberries. Spoon into nonstick muffin cups. Sprinkle the tops with sugar. Bake at 375 degrees for 25 minutes or until the muffins test done.

Note: Can reduce the butter to 1/4 cup (1/2 stick) and add 1/4 cup unsweetened applesauce to reduce the fat content.

Beachside Banana Bread

Yield: 12 servings

1/2 cup (1 stick) butter, softened
1 cup sugar
2 eggs
2 or 3 ripe bananas, mashed
2 cups flour
1 teaspoon baking soda
1 teaspoon salt
1 teaspoon vanilla extract

Beat the butter and sugar in a mixer bowl until light and fluffy. Add the eggs and bananas and mix well. Add the flour, baking soda, salt and vanilla and mix until blended. Spoon into a greased 5x9-inch loaf pan.

Bake at 350 degrees for 1 hour or until a wooden pick inserted in the center comes out clean.

Note: May add chocolate chips or nuts to this recipe. For muffins, spoon the batter into 12 muffin cups. Bake at 375 degrees for 20 to 25 minutes or until the muffins test done.

Smiling Hill Farm Eggnog Bread

Yield: 12 servings

2³/4 cups flour
³/4 cup sugar
1   tablespoon baking powder
1   teaspoon salt
¹/2 teaspoon mace

1¹/2 cups eggnog
¹/4 cup (¹/2 stick) butter, melted
1   egg, beaten
1   tablespoon rum
³/4 cup chopped pecans

Mix the flour, sugar, baking powder, salt and mace in a large bowl. Add the eggnog, butter, egg and rum and stir just until moistened; the batter will be lumpy. Fold in the pecans. Spoon into a greased 5x9-inch loaf pan. Bake at 350 degrees for 1 hour or until the loaf tests done. Cool in the pan for 10 minutes. Invert onto a wire rack to cool completely.

Note: This bread freezes well.

*Smiling Hill Farm in Westbrook is one of the oldest vendors of the Portland Public Market.
It has been owned and operated by the Knight family since the early eighteenth
century. The farm has over one hundred purebred black and white Holstein dairy
cows and a creamery that bottles milk.*

Best-Ever Pumpkin Bread

Yield: 24 servings

3 1/3 cups flour, sifted
3 cups sugar
2 teaspoons baking soda
1 1/2 teaspoons salt
1 teaspoon cinnamon
1 teaspoon nutmeg

- Pinch of ground cloves
4 eggs
1 cup vegetable oil
2/3 cup water
1 (16-ounce) can pumpkin

Sift the flour, sugar, baking soda, salt, cinnamon, nutmeg and cloves together. Beat the eggs, vegetable oil, water and pumpkin in a mixer bowl until blended. Add the flour mixture and mix until moistened. Pour into 2 greased 5x9-inch loaf pans. Bake at 350 degrees for 50 to 60 minutes or until the loaves test done.

Note: May add raisins, nuts and/or coconut.

Believe-It-or-Not Beer Bread

Yield: 24 servings

This recipe was written on the back of an old wine list by the chef at Westways on Kezar Lake. It is best eaten when warm and freshly baked.

6 cups flour
6 tablespoons sugar
2 tablespoons baking powder

1 tablespoon salt
2 (12-ounce) cans beer
1 tablespoon butter

Combine the flour, sugar, baking powder and salt in a food processor container. Add the beer in a fine stream, processing constantly. Spoon into 2 buttered 5x9-inch loaf pans. Bake at 375 degrees for 40 minutes. Spread the top of each loaf with 1/2 the butter. Bake for 20 to 25 minutes longer or until the loaves test done.

Note: May reduce the ingredients by 1/2 to make 1 loaf.

Swedish Rye Bread

Yield: 4 round loaves

3	cups milk	1/2	cup packed brown sugar
1/4	cup (1/2 stick) margarine	1	cup molasses
2	envelopes dry yeast	2	cups rye flour
1	teaspoon sugar	2	teaspoons anise seeds
3/4	cup lukewarm water	2	teaspoons salt
2	eggs	10	to 12 cups bread flour

Heat the milk and margarine in a saucepan over medium-high heat until the margarine is melted, stirring to mix; do not boil. Cool slightly.

Dissolve the yeast and sugar in the water in a bowl. Let stand until foamy.

Combine the milk mixture, eggs, brown sugar, molasses, rye flour, anise seeds, salt and yeast mixture in a large bowl and mix well. Stir in enough of the bread flour to form a dough that is firm enough to handle. Let rest, covered, for 10 minutes.

Knead on a lightly floured surface for 10 minutes. Place in a greased bowl, turning to coat the surface. Let rise for 1 1/2 to 2 hours. Punch the dough down. Divide into 4 portions. Let rest for 10 minutes. Shape into round loaves. Place on a nonstick baking sheet. Let rise for 1 to 1 1/2 hours. Bake at 375 degrees for 30 minutes, being careful not to let the tops burn.

Note: The dough may be divided into 3 portions. Shape into loaves and place in nonstick 5x9-inch loaf pans. Bake at 375 degrees for 45 minutes.

Magnum Opus
Entrées

Magnum Opus

Entrées

Red Clam Stew

Yield: 8 to 10 servings

A hearty dinner to serve to a group.

4   (28-ounce) cans peeled plum tomatoes
8   to 12 fresh plum tomatoes, chopped
6   large onions, coarsely chopped
3   large red bell peppers, chopped
1   to 1¹/₂ cups coarsely chopped fresh parsley
1   to 1¹/₂ cups coarsely chopped fresh dill
6   to 10 garlic cloves, coarsely chopped
1   tablespoon fennel seeds
1   tablespoon anise seeds
2   to 3 tablespoons oregano
1   tablespoon angostura bitters
•   Salt and pepper to taste
2   (28-ounce) cans baby clams

Drain the juice from the canned tomatoes into a large stockpot. Chop the canned tomatoes and add to the stockpot. Add the fresh tomatoes, onions, red peppers, parsley, dill, garlic, fennel seeds, anise seeds, oregano, angostura bitters, salt and pepper and mix well. Cook over medium heat until the vegetables are tender. Add the clams. Cook until heated through. Do not overcook. Serve with bagels or a favorite bread.

Steamed Soft-Shell Clams

Yield: 4 servings

Found mostly north of Cape Cod, these clams can be dug from mud or sandy clam flats. Their shell color can range from black to white depending on the kind of mud they are found in. Mud clams are usually darker in color than sand clams.

8 to 12 pounds fresh clams	• Chopped shallots
1 gallon water	• Salt and pepper to taste
$^1\!/_2$ cup vinegar	• Lemon juice
• Chopped onion	• Seaweed
• Chopped celery	• White wine
• Chopped fresh parsley	• Bay leaf
• Chopped garlic	

Rinse the clams. Combine 1 gallon of water and vinegar in a large container. Add the clams. Let stand for 1 hour. Rinse the clams again.

Place 3 to 5 inches of water in a large stockpot. Add the onion, celery, parsley, garlic, shallots, salt and pepper, lemon juice, seaweed, white wine and bay leaf in desired amounts. Add the clams. Steam over medium heat until the clams open. Place the clams in soup bowls. Serve with a small dish of melted butter or Huckleberry Island Sauce (page 101).

To eat the clams, pick up the clams by the neck, removing the black "beard." Dip into the broth to remove any sand and then dip into the butter. The broth is delicious to drink, but to avoid any residual sand, do not entirely drain the cup.

Note: Allow 2 to 3 pounds of clams per person.

Huckleberry Island Sauce

Yield: 8 servings

- Juice of 2 lemons
- 3 tablespoons white wine vinegar
- 1/4 cup Worcestershire sauce
- 1 tablespoon Dijon mustard
- Tabasco sauce to taste
- 1 pound (4 sticks) butter

Combine the lemon juice, white wine vinegar, Worcestershire sauce, Dijon mustard and Tabasco sauce in a heavy 1-quart saucepan and mix well. Simmer over low heat until heated through. Add the butter a small amount at a time, stirring constantly until the sauce has a creamy consistency. Serve hot with steamed clams.

Clam Chowder Pie

Yield: 4 to 6 servings

- 2 medium potatoes, peeled, chopped
- 2 (8-ounce) cans chopped clams, drained
- 4 teaspoons flour
- 1/4 cup chopped onion
- 2 tablespoons (1/4 stick) margarine, melted
- 2 tablespoons parsley flakes
- 1 unbaked (10-inch) pie shell

Combine the potatoes, clams, flour, onion, melted margarine and parsley flakes in a bowl and mix well. Pour into the pie shell. Bake at 350 degrees for 30 minutes.

Crab Meat and Shrimp Casserole

Yield: 6 to 10 servings

Great recipe to serve for parties and special occasions.

1	green bell pepper, finely chopped	1/4	teaspoon pepper
1	onion, finely chopped	2	tablespoons Worcestershire sauce
1	cup finely chopped celery	1 1/2	cups mayonnaise
1	pound shrimp, peeled, deveined	1 1/2	cups bread crumbs
1	pound crab meat, flaked		

Combine the green pepper, onion, celery, shrimp, crab meat, pepper, Worcestershire sauce and mayonnaise in a bowl and mix well. Spread in a greased 9x13-inch baking dish. Sprinkle the bread crumbs on top. Bake at 350 degrees for 30 minutes.

Wine Suggestion: Riesling with citrus notes to complement the shellfish or a Viognier

Old-Fashioned Crab Cakes

Yield: 8 servings

2	pounds crab meat, flaked	•	Dash of cayenne pepper
2	eggs	1/4	teaspoon celery salt
2	tablespoons mayonnaise	3	tablespoons cracker meal
1	teaspoon chopped fresh parsley	1	tablespoon chopped pimento
1	teaspoon dry mustard	•	Seafood seasoning to taste
•	Dash of Worcestershire sauce	2	to 3 tablespoons butter

Combine the crab meat, eggs, mayonnaise, parsley, dry mustard, Worcestershire sauce, cayenne pepper, celery salt, cracker meal and pimento in a bowl and mix well. Shape into 16 patties. Sprinkle each side of the patties with seafood seasoning.

Melt the butter in a 12-inch skillet. Add the crab meat patties. Cook for 3 to 4 minutes on each side or until golden brown.

Wine Suggestion: Light young Chardonnay

Lobster Facts

Lobsters are found along a 1,300-mile-long area in the Atlantic Ocean between Cape Hatteras and Labrador. Along the rocky coast of Maine are found the choicest specimens. In 1994 over thirty-eight million pounds of lobsters were caught, more than half of all lobsters caught in the United States.

A female lobster lays up to 100,000 eggs at a time, but only 100 of those will live longer than six weeks.

An adult lobster will shed its old shell and grow a new one once or twice a year, increasing about $1/2$ inch and $1/3$ pound each time. It takes about eight weeks for the new shell to harden. This process is known as molting. It occurs during the summer, and it is a full six months before the new shell hardens completely. These soft-shell lobsters are commonly found in Maine in July and August.

It takes a lobster four to seven years to grow to be one pound in weight and become an adult. During that time, the lobster molts about 25 times. Generally they live about fifteen years. However, in 1977 a Canadian lobster that weighed $44^1/2$ pounds was caught. It was estimated to be 100 years old.

The longest lobster ever caught in Maine measured 36 inches from nose to tail. The largest lobster ever caught weighed forty-two pounds, seven ounces.

Lobsters do not spoil for ten to twelve hours after they die, assuming that they have been kept cold, and dead lobsters can be cooked and eaten safely. If you do not detect an ammonia odor after cooking the lobster, it is edible.

Lobster is very high in amino acids, which are the building blocks of protein. They are also high in potassium and magnesium; vitamins A, B12, B6, B3, and B2; calcium; zinc; and iron. Lobster also contains omega-3 fatty acids, which are known to decrease the risk of heart disease.

Lobsters were once so plentiful in Maine that they could be found on the beaches live after a strong Nor'easter. Back then the average lobster weighed between five and fifteen pounds. So commonly disparaged was the lobster that Massachusetts even passed a law stipulating that servants in a household could not be served lobster more than three times a week. However, by the early 1800s public tastes shifted and lobster came into vogue. Napoleon is said to have celebrated a battlefield victory with savory Lobster Thermador. Queen Victoria served lobster with hollandaise sauce on many party menus.

Lobsters crawl around on the ocean floor feeding on weaker, smaller lobsters, but, like humans, they also enjoy crab, clams, and fresh cod.

Maine Lobster Bake

Yield: 4 servings

12	small red Maine potatoes, scrubbed	4	ears sweet corn, shucked except for the innermost leaves
2	quarts water	2	pounds mussels, cleaned
4	small boiling onions, peeled	2	pounds steamer clams, cleaned
5	pounds seaweed	2	cups water
4	(1- to 1¹/4-pound) live Maine lobsters	1	cup (2 sticks) butter, melted
		2	lemons, quartered lengthwise

Parboil the potatoes in 2 quarts boiling water in a 4-to 6-quart stockpot for 5 minutes. Add the onions. Parboil for 2 minutes; drain.

Place a layer of seaweed 1 inch thick evenly in a 12x16-inch roasting pan. Lay the lobsters on top of the seaweed. Arrange the corn and onions between the lobsters and sides of pan. Place a thin layer of seaweed over the lobsters, corn and onions. Layer the mussels, clams and parboiled potatoes over the top, making sure the top is level. Cover with the remaining seaweed. Add 2 cups water. Cover the roasting pan tightly with a lid or foil.

Cook over high heat or grill over very hot coals. Cook for 15 minutes, beginning to time at the first sign of steam. Remove from the heat. Let stand, covered, for 5 minutes. Serve immediately with melted butter and lemon wedges.

Note: If seaweed is unavailable, add 2 teaspoons salt to water and use a low rack to keep the lobsters off the bottom of the roasting pan.

Buttery Lobster Casserole

Yield: 6 servings

1 cup cracker crumbs	12 ounces mushrooms
1/4 cup chopped onions	1 to 2 green onions, thinly sliced
1/2 cup (1 stick) butter, melted	2 pounds cooked lobster meat, cut into bite-size pieces
• Parsley, thyme and paprika to taste	3/4 cup shredded Monterey Jack cheese or Cheddar cheese
1/4 cup butter (1/2 stick) butter	2 tablespoons (1/4 stick) butter
1 garlic clove, minced	

Process the cracker crumbs, onions, 1/2 cup butter, parsley, thyme and paprika in a blender until mixed.

Melt 1/4 cup butter in a small skillet. Add the garlic, mushrooms and green onions. Sauté until soft. Add the lobster and toss well.

Place the lobster mixture in a baking dish. Sprinkle with the cracker crumb mixture. Sprinkle the cheese over the top. Dot with 2 tablespoons butter. Bake at 400 degrees for 15 minutes or until the cheese is melted and the lobster is heated through. Do not overcook.

Note: May assemble ahead of time and bake just before serving. Make sure the lobster is cool or it will dry out during baking.

Wine Suggestion: A chilled white Burgundy or a full-bodied Chardonnay

Approximately 7,000 licensed Maine lobster harvesters now supply 400 dealers and wholesalers within the state. The annual catch during each of the last five years has been over thirty-six million pounds with a value of over $100 million each year.

Long Island Lobster Casserole

Yield: 4 servings

1 pound lobster meat, cut into bite-size pieces	2 cups milk
3 tablespoons butter	1 tablespoon sherry
3 tablespoons flour	3 slices white bread, crusts trimmed, torn into bite-size pieces
3/4 teaspoon dry mustard	
• Salt and pepper to taste	• Buttered cracker crumbs

Cook the lobster in the butter in a skillet over low heat until the lobster turns pink. Do not cook too long or too fast, or the lobster will become tough. Remove the lobster to a bowl using a slotted spoon.

Season the flour with dry mustard, salt and pepper to taste. Add to the pan drippings in the skillet. Stir in the milk gradually. Cook until thickened, stirring constantly. Add the sherry, lobster and bread and mix well. Spoon into a buttered baking dish. Sprinkle with buttered cracker crumbs. Bake at 350 degrees for 30 minutes or until brown and bubbly.

Note: May add scallops.

Lobster Newburg

Yield: 4 servings

1/4 cup (1/2 stick) butter	2 cups milk or light cream
12 ounces cooked lobster meat, cubed	2 egg yolks, beaten
1/2 teaspoon paprika	2 tablespoons sherry
3 tablespoons flour	• Salt and pepper to taste

Melt the butter in a double boiler over boiling water. Add the lobster and paprika. Heat for 3 minutes or until the lobster is warm and the butter turns red. Remove from the heat. Add the flour and blend well. Stir in 1 1/2 cups milk gradually. Cook over boiling water until thickened and smooth, stirring constantly. Do not boil. Stir in a mixture of the remaining milk and egg yolks. Cook until thickened and smooth, stirring constantly. Stir in the sherry. Season with salt and pepper. Serve over toast points or patty shells.

Wine Suggestion: A light Sancerre or a fully chilled Albariño

Lobster Fra Diavolo

Yield: 2 servings

Serve with crusty bread, white wine and a roll of paper towels.

2/3	cup water	1/4	teaspoon oregano
2/3	cup white wine	1/8	teaspoon hot red pepper flakes, or to taste
2	live lobsters	•	Salt, pepper and red pepper flakes to taste
2	tablespoons olive oil		
3	large garlic cloves, minced	8	ounces linguini
1	(28- or 32-ounce) can crushed tomatoes	1	tablespoon chopped fresh parsley

Heat the water and white wine in a large stockpot over high heat until steaming. Add the lobsters and cover. Steam for 2 to 3 minutes or until partially cooked. Remove the lobsters to a platter. Cook the liquid in the stockpot until reduced by 1/2.

Heat the olive oil in a Dutch oven or large skillet. Add the garlic. Sauté until light brown. Add the tomatoes. Stir in the oregano and 1/8 teaspoon red pepper flakes. Bring to a simmer. Add the lobster liquid. Simmer until thickened, stirring frequently.

Split the lobsters down the center. Remove the sac behind the head, the entrails and the vein in the tail. Crack the claws and knuckles. Place the lobsters in the sauce. Simmer, partially covered, until the lobsters just turn bright red and the sauce is thickened, turning the lobsters occasionally and ladling the sauce over the lobsters. Add salt, pepper and red pepper flakes to taste. Continue cooking until the lobster meat is opaque.

Cook the linguini in boiling salted water in a saucepan until al dente; drain. Place the linguini on serving plates. Ladle the sauce over the linguini. Place a lobster over the top of each. Sprinkle with chopped parsley.

Note: May cut the lobster meat into pieces if desired.

Wine Suggestion: A light style Petite Syrah or a more adventurous oaky Zinfandel.

Mussels with Cream Sauce

Yield: 2 to 4 servings

2	pounds mussels	$1/2$	cup heavy cream
3	tablespoons unsalted butter	$1/4$	teaspoon yellow Indian curry
3	large garlic cloves, minced		powder (optional)
$1/2$	cup white wine	2	tablespoons finely chopped
1	tablespoon unsalted butter		fresh parsley

Rinse, debeard and scrub the mussels under cold running water, discarding any broken mussels. Melt 3 tablespoons butter in a skillet over medium heat. Add the garlic. Sauté until light brown. Add the wine and mussels and toss to coat.

Steam, covered, over medium-high heat for 3 to 5 minutes or until the mussels open. Do not overcook. Remove the mussels to a bowl using a slotted spoon, discarding any mussels that did not open. Cover the bowl with foil and keep warm.

Bring the liquid in the skillet to a boil. Cook until it is reduced by $1/2$. Add 1 tablespoon butter, cream and curry powder. Cook until thickened, stirring constantly.

To serve, place the mussels in serving bowls. Pour some of the sauce over the mussels. Sprinkle with parsley. Serve the remaining sauce for dipping.

Wine Suggestion: A crisp, dry white Bordeaux

Scalloped Oysters

Yield: 4 servings

1	quart oysters with liquor	1	teaspoon salt
1	cup soft bread crumbs	•	Dash of pepper
1^1/2	cups fine dry cracker crumbs	•	Dash of nutmeg
^{3}/4	cup (1^1/2 sticks) butter, melted	^{1}/4	cup milk
2	tablespoons chopped fresh parsley		

Drain the oysers, reserving ^{1}/2 cup of the liquor. Mix the bread crumbs, cracker crumbs and melted butter in a bowl. Line the bottom of a greased baking dish with ^{1}/2 of the crumb mixture. Arrange the oysters in 3 layers in the prepared dish, sprinkling each layer with parsley, salt, pepper and nutmeg. Add the reserved oyster liquor and milk. Top with the remaining crumb mixture. Bake at 350 degrees for 1 hour or until puffed and brown.

Note: May double the recipe.

Casco Bay Scallops in Vermouth Sauce

Yield: 4 servings

1^1/2	pounds scallops	3	tablespoons flour
2	cups sliced mushrooms	1	cup skim milk
1	garlic clove, minced	^{1}/2	cup dry vermouth
2	teaspoons olive oil	•	Salt and pepper to taste
2	teaspoons butter		

Sauté the scallops, mushrooms and garlic in the hot olive oil and butter in a skillet until the scallops begin to brown and the mushrooms are tender. Remove to a large baking dish with a slotted spoon.

Blend the flour into the pan drippings in the skillet. Add the milk and whisk well. Cook until thickened and smooth, whisking constantly. Reduce the heat. Add the vermouth gradually, stirring constantly. Season with salt and pepper. Spread over the scallops and mushrooms in the baking dish. Broil until brown.

Wine Suggestion: Chenin Blanc

Grilled Garlic Shrimp

Yield: 6 servings

6	garlic cloves, minced	2	tablespoons lemon juice
3/4	cup (1 1/2 sticks) butter, melted	•	Freshly ground pepper to taste
3/4	cup olive oil	36	jumbo shrimp, peeled, butterflied
1/4	cup minced parsley		

Combine the garlic, butter, olive oil, parsley, lemon juice and pepper in a bowl. Add the shrimp and mix well. Marinate, covered, in the refrigerator for 4 hours or longer. Drain the shrimp, reserving the marinade. Bring the reserved marinade to a boil in a saucepan. Boil for 2 to 3 minutes. Remove from the heat. Reserve some of the heated marinade for dipping.

Place the marinated shrimp in a grilling basket or on foil. Grill for 5 minutes or until the shrimp turn pink, basting with the remaining heated marinade. Serve with the reserved heated marinade for dipping.

Wine Suggestion: Fumé Blanc

Barbecued Shrimp

Yield: 2 to 4 servings

12	whole fresh basil leaves	6	thin slices prosciutto, cut into halves lengthwise
12	large shrimp with tails, peeled, deveined		

Wrap a basil leaf around the middle of each shrimp. Wrap a piece of prosciutto around each, cutting off any excess and securing with a soaked wooden pick. Place on an oiled grill rack. Grill over hot coals until the shrimp turn pink, turning once. Do not overcook.

Variation: Place the shrimp in a mixture of 1/4 cup extra-virgin olive oil, 1 1/2 teaspoons lemon juice, 1 garlic clove, minced, and 1/2 teaspoon grated Parmesan cheese in a bowl. Marinate, covered, in the refrigerator for 20 minutes, turning once. Shake off the excess marinade and wrap as above.

Curried Shrimp with Grand Marnier Sauce

Yield: 6 to 8 servings

Delicious and elegant entrée.

2 pounds medium shrimp, peeled, deveined	1 tablespoon curry powder
1/4 cup vegetable oil	1/2 cup Grand Marnier
1 onion, finely chopped	1 1/3 cups chicken broth
2 tablespoons minced garlic	2/3 cup heavy cream
1 tablespoon chopped fresh gingerroot	1 tablespoon lime juice
	• Pepper to taste

Sauté the shrimp in the vegetable oil in a skillet in 2 separate batches just until pink. Transfer to a bowl. Add the onion to the skillet. Sauté over low heat until softened. Add the garlic, gingerroot and curry powder. Cook for 2 minutes. Add the Grand Marnier. Boil until the liquid is evaporated. Add the chicken broth. Cook until reduced by 2/3. Add the cream. Boil until syrupy. Add the shrimp, lime juice and pepper to taste. Simmer until heated through. Serve over rice.

Sweet Maine Shrimp de Jonghe

Yield: 4 servings

6   tablespoons (3/4 stick) butter
2   scallions, chopped
1   garlic clove, minced
1   pound Maine shrimp, peeled, deveined

2/3   sleeve butter crackers, crushed (approximately 27 crackers)

Melt the butter in a 2-quart saucepan over medium heat. Add the scallions, garlic and shrimp and mix well. Remove from the heat. Add the cracker crumbs and toss to coat. Spread in a 2-quart baking dish. Bake at 350 degrees for 25 minutes.

Kettle Cove Crab and Shrimp Casserole

Yield: 6 servings

1   or 2 cups canned shrimp, drained
1   or 2 cups canned crab meat, drained
1   or 2 (7-ounce) cans minced clams, drained
2   cups chopped celery
1/2   cup chopped green onions
1   (10-ounce) can cream of mushroom soup

1   (8-ounce) can bamboo shoots, drained (optional)
1   (8-ounce) can water chestnuts, drained (optional)
1   cup chopped fresh or canned mushrooms
1   large can Chinese noodles

Combine the shrimp, crab meat, clams, celery, green onions, mushroom soup, bamboo shoots, water chestnuts and mushrooms in a large bowl and mix well. Spoon into a 9x13-inch baking dish. Top with the Chinese noodles. Bake at 350 degrees for 30 minutes.

Mount Desert Seafood Casserole

Yield: 21 servings

3/4 cup (1 1/2 sticks) butter
1 pound (or more) cooked lobster meat chunks
1 pound medium shrimp, peeled, deveined
1 pound scallops
3/4 cup flour
2 1/4 teaspoons dry mustard

1 1/2 quarts cream
15 slices white bread, crusts trimmed
• Salt and paprika to taste
1/2 cup cooking sherry
• Butter crackers, crushed
• Melted butter

Melt 3/4 cup butter in a large skillet. Add the lobster meat, shrimp and scallops. Sauté for 5 minutes or until tender. Do not overcook. Sprinkle flour and dry mustard over the seafood. Add enough of the cream to fill the skillet. Cook until thickened, stirring constantly.

Tear the bread into pieces in a large bowl. Add the remaining cream. Stir in the seafood mixture. Season with salt and paprika. Add the cooking sherry. Spoon into a greased large shallow baking pan. Sprinkle with a mixture of the crushed crackers and melted butter. Bake at 325 degrees for 40 to 50 minutes or until hot and bubbly.

Tortellini with Seafood Sauce

Yield: 4 servings

- 1/4 cup (1/2 stick) butter
- 1/2 cup dry white wine
- 1 garlic clove, chopped
- 1 pound fresh seafood
- 1 cup half-and-half
- 3/4 cup grated Parmesan cheese
- • Salt to taste
- • Pinch of nutmeg
- 1/4 teaspoon pepper
- 1/4 cup chopped fresh parsley
- 8 ounces spinach tortellini, cooked, drained

Melt the butter in a skillet. Add the wine and garlic. Sauté until the mixture is reduced to 1/3 cup. Add the seafood. Cook for 2 minutes. Add the cream. Simmer for 2 minutes. Add the Parmesan cheese, salt, nutmeg, pepper and parsley. Spoon over the tortellini in individual serving bowls.

Note: Any fresh seafood is good to use in this recipe. A combination of small shrimp, scallops and chopped haddock would be an excellent choice.

Poached Fish Fillets with Soy Dressing

Yield: 4 servings

This is a Chinese way of cooking fish. It is important to not overcook the fish.
The amounts of the sauce ingredients may be adjusted to taste.

1¹/2 pounds (³/4-inch-thick) firm
white fish, such as haddock, cod,
halibut or bass
- Salt to taste
¹/2 tablespoon salt
2 tablespoons thinly sliced fresh
gingerroot

4 green onions, cut into halves
horizontally, cut into halves
lengthwise
2 tablespoons fresh cilantro or
coriander sprigs
- Soy Dressing

Sprinkle the fish generously with salt. Let stand for 5 minutes. Pour water to a depth of 2 inches in a large skillet. Add ¹/2 tablespoon salt and a few gingerroot pieces. Bring to a boil and reduce the heat. Add the fish. Simmer, covered, for 5 minutes or until the fish is opaque. Remove the fish to a serving platter using a slotted spoon. Sprinkle with the remaining gingerroot pieces, green onions and cilantro.

Drizzle the Soy Dressing over the fish. Serve immediately.

Soy Dressing

3 tablespoons soy sauce
2 tablespoons shao-hsing wine or
dry sherry

1 tablespoon peanut oil

Bring the soy sauce, wine and peanut oil to a boil in a small saucepan.

Old Port Party Fish

Yield: 6 servings

2 (10-ounce) packages frozen chopped spinach, thawed, drained
2 pounds haddock
2 cups sour cream
$1/2$ cup mayonnaise
$1/2$ teaspoon pepper
$1/4$ teaspoon thyme
2 tablespoons fresh dill, or 1 teaspoon dried dill
• Fresh lemon slices

Place the thawed spinach in a buttered baking dish. Arrange the fish over the spinach. Combine the sour cream, mayonnaise, pepper and thyme in a bowl and mix well. Pour over the fish.

Bake at 350 degrees for 30 to 40 minutes or until the fish flakes easily. Sprinkle with the dill and lemon slices.

Note: May substitute fresh spinach for the frozen spinach.

Atlantic Haddock

Yield: variable

- Haddock
- Mayonnaise
- Thousand Island salad dressing

- Milk
- Bread crumbs
- Salt and pepper to taste

Place the fish in a baking dish. Mix equal parts of mayonnaise and salad dressing in a bowl. Spread over the top of the fish. Add enough milk to come 1/3 the way up the side of the fish. Sprinkle the fish with bread crumbs and salt and pepper. Bake at 350 degrees for 30 minutes or until the fish flakes easily.

Note: May substitute catsup or Dijon mustard for the salad dressing. May also drizzle melted butter over the bread crumbs.

The American humorist Artemus Ward, born Charles Farrar Browne in Waterville, Maine, was a favorite of Abraham Lincoln. An example of his Maine wit: "I am not a politician and my other habits are also good."

Salmon in Parchment

Yield: 4 servings

Serve this low-calorie recipe with boiled red potatoes, a green salad and hot rolls.

1 large leek bulb	$1/2$ teaspoon salt
2 medium carrots	$1/4$ teaspoon pepper
1 medium red bell pepper	4 fresh dill sprigs
$1^1/2$ tablespoons olive oil	
4 (6-ounce) portions fresh salmon, 1 to $1^1/2$ inches thick	

Cut the leek bulb into halves and rinse with water. Cut the leek bulb halves, carrots and red pepper into thin strips 3 inches long. Sauté the vegetable strips in hot olive oil in a 10-inch skillet over medium heat for 3 minutes or until tender-crisp.

Place 1 salmon portion in the center of a 12-inch square of baking parchment. Sprinkle the salmon with salt and pepper. Add $1/4$ of the vegetable mixture. Top with 1 dill sprig. Bring 2 sides of the parchment together and fold to enclose the salmon; tuck under the short sides to seal. Place on a baking sheet. Repeat with the remaining salmon. Bake at 400 degrees for 20 minutes. Unwrap and place on serving plates.

Note: May prepare the salmon packets ahead of time and store in the refrigerator. Remove 30 to 60 minutes before baking.

Cold Poached Salmon with Avocado Sauce

Yield: 4 servings

2 tablespoons minced shallots
4 (8-ounce) salmon steaks,
   1 inch thick
• Salt and freshly ground pepper
   to taste

1 tablespoon butter, cut into pieces
1¼ cups fish stock
• Avocado Sauce

Sprinkle 1 tablespoon shallots in a baking dish. Season the fish with salt and pepper. Arrange in a single layer over the shallots. Dot with butter. Sprinkle with the remaining shallots.

Bring the fish stock to a boil in a saucepan. Pour over the fish. Cover with a buttered piece of waxed paper. Bake at 350 degrees for 15 minutes. Remove from the oven. Let stand, covered, until cool. Uncover and remove with a slotted spoon to a serving plate. Spoon some of the Avocado Sauce over the fish. Serve with the remaining Avocado Sauce.

Note: May substitute white wine and water for the fish stock.

Avocado Sauce

1 large ripe avocado
½ cup light mayonnaise
2 tablespoons lemon juice
¼ teaspoon Tabasco sauce

1 garlic clove, minced
1 green onion, finely minced
• Salt and pepper to taste

Mash the avocado in a bowl. Add the mayonnaise, lemon juice and Tabasco sauce and mix well. Stir in the garlic and green onion. Season with salt and pepper. Adjust the seasonings if needed.

Savory Salmon Pie

Yield: 4 to 6 servings

1	(16-ounce) can red salmon	2	cups cooked rice
2	eggs	1	(8-ounce) can tomato sauce
1/4	cup chopped onion	1/2	teaspoon oregano
1/4	cup chopped green bell pepper	1 1/2	cups shredded sharp Cheddar
1/2	cup bread crumbs		cheese
1/4	teaspoon lemon pepper		

Drain the salmon. Flake the salmon, discarding the skin and bone. Mash the salmon in a bowl. Add the eggs, onion, green pepper, bread crumbs and lemon pepper and mix well. Line a greased 9-inch pie plate with the salmon mixture, fluting the edge.

Combine the rice, tomato sauce, oregano and 1 cup of the Cheddar cheese in a bowl and mix well. Spoon into the salmon shell. Cover with foil. Bake at 350 degrees for 25 minutes. Remove the foil. Sprinkle with the remaining Cheddar cheese. Bake, uncovered, for 10 to 15 minutes or until the pie is set and the cheese is melted. Cool for a few minutes before serving.

Wine Suggestion: Chablis

The annual fish catch for Maine is valued at $272 million. Lobster landed value is $137 million, followed by Atlantic salmon at $49 million, and sea urchins at $20 million.

Grilled Lemon Dill Salmon

Yield: 6 servings

2	tablespoons dill	2	tablespoons white wine vinegar
1	teaspoon garlic powder	•	Juice of 2 lemons
1/4	teaspoon Beau Monde seasoning	1 1/2	to 2 pounds salmon fillets or
1/4	cup olive oil		steaks

Combine the dillweed, garlic powder, Beau Monde seasoning, olive oil, white wine vinegar and lemon juice in a bowl and mix well. Pour over the salmon in a shallow dish. Marinate, covered, in the refrigerator for 2 hours or longer, turning once. Drain the salmon, reserving the marinade.

Place the reserved marinade in a saucepan. Boil for 2 to 3 minutes and remove from the heat.

Place the salmon on a grill rack. Grill until the salmon flakes easily, basting with the heated reserved marinade.

Scrod à la Maison

Yield: 4 servings

4	(6-ounce) scrod fillets	•	Salt and pepper to taste
1/3	cup mayonnaise	1	cup fine bread crumbs
1/3	cup buttermilk	•	Paprika to taste
1 1/2	tablespoons fresh lemon juice		
1	garlic clove, pressed or finely minced		

Rinse the fish and pat dry. Combine the mayonnaise, buttermilk, lemon juice, garlic, salt and pepper in a bowl and mix well. Spread the bread crumbs on a plate or sheet of waxed paper.

Dip each fillet in the mayonnaise mixture, letting the excess drip off. Place in the bread crumbs, turning to coat. Roll up the fillets to an even thickness. Place in a shallow baking dish. Sprinkle with paprika. Bake at 450 degrees for 12 to 15 minutes or until crisp and the fish flakes easily. Serve with lemon wedges.

Note: May be prepared ahead and baked just before serving.

Wine Suggestion: Sémillion

Brisket with Carrots and String Beans

Yield: 4 to 6 servings

3	to 3½ pounds brisket	3	to 4 garlic cloves, chopped
•	Salt and freshly ground pepper to taste	1	(16-ounce) can tomato sauce
•	Paprika to taste	2	to 4 medium carrots, sliced
1	medium onion, finely chopped	2	cups cut string beans

Season the brisket with salt, pepper and paprika on both sides. Sear the brisket on all sides in a Dutch oven. Add the chopped onion, garlic, tomato sauce and a small amount of water. Simmer, covered, for 1½ hours. Remove the brisket to a platter. Trim and cut into slices. Return the brisket to the Dutch oven. Add the carrots and beans. Cook, covered, for 1½ to 2 hours or until the brisket is tender.

EATING LOBSTER

First twist off the large claws. Crack each claw and knuckle with a nutcracker or pliers. Remove the meat. Separate the tail from the body and break off the tail flippers. Don't overlook the small amount of meat in each flipper. Insert a fork and push out the tail meat in one piece. Remove and discard the black vein that runs the entire length of the tail meat. Separate the shell from the underside by pulling it apart; discard the green substance called the tomalley. Open the underside of the body by cracking it apart in the middle with the little legs on either side. Lobster meat lies in the four pockets or joints, where the small walking legs are attached. These walking legs also contain wonderful meat that can be removed by biting down on the leg and squeezing the meat out with your teeth.

Authentic Viennese Beef Goulash

Yield: 4 to 6 servings

From the podium of Maestro Toshiyuki Shimada

1 tablespoon vegetable oil	1 (16-ounce) can peeled tomatoes, chopped
2 cups finely chopped onions	1 chicken bouillon cube
2 garlic cloves, finely chopped	1/2 tablespoon sugar
2 pounds beef round or any stew beef, cut into 1¹/₂-inch pieces	3 cups water
2 teaspoons caraway seeds	2 medium Yukon Gold potatoes, peeled, cut into 1¹/₂-inch pieces
1 tablespoon crushed marjoram	2 tablespoons flour
1 medium green bell pepper, finely chopped (optional)	2 tablespoons water
1 tablespoon Hungarian paprika	• Salt and pepper to taste
1 tablespoon flour	

Heat the vegetable oil in a large heavy saucepan. Add the onions and garlic. Sauté until transparent. Add the beef, caraway seeds, marjoram and green pepper. Sauté until the beef is light brown. Add paprika and 1 tablespoon flour and mix well to coat. Add the tomatoes, bouillon cube, sugar and 3 cups water. Bring to a boil.

Simmer, partially covered, for 1 hour or until the beef is almost tender. Add the potatoes. Cook for 20 minutes or until the potatoes are tender. Stir in a mixture of 2 tablespoons flour and 2 tablespoons water. Cook until thickened, stirring constantly. Season with salt and pepper.

Sweetbreads with Cream Sauce

Yield: 4 servings

1¹/₂ pounds sweetbreads
¹/₂ cup plus 1 tablespoon chopped fresh parsley
¹/₂ cup chopped onion
• Pinch of salt
• Pinch of white pepper
2 cups chicken stock
1¹/₂ cups Cream Sauce
2 hard-cooked eggs, chopped
¹/₄ cup sherry

Boil the sweetbreads in water to cover in a saucepan until tender. Cool and remove the skin. Combine with parsley, onions, salt and white pepper in a saucepan. Add the chicken stock. Cook until tender. Remove from the heat. Add the Cream Sauce and mix well. Stir in the eggs and sherry. Place in a double boiler over warm water until serving time.

Cream Sauce

2 tablespoons (¹/₄ stick) butter
2 tablespoons flour
¹/₄ teaspoon salt
• Pinch of pepper
1 cup milk or light cream

Melt the butter in a small saucepan. Mix the flour, salt and pepper in a bowl. Blend the flour mixture into the melted butter. Add the milk gradually, stirring constantly. Bring just to the boiling point. Cook for 2 to 3 minutes or until thickened, stirring constantly.

Curried Shepherd Pie

Yield: 4 to 8 servings

This is true comfort food and is a welcome addition to any potluck gathering.

2 tablespoons (1/4 stick) butter	8 ounces fresh or frozen sliced green beans, cooked
1 large onion, chopped	
2 pounds lean ground beef or lamb	8 ounces fresh or frozen green peas, cooked
1/4 cup flour	
1 tablespoon curry powder, or to taste	8 ounces fresh or frozen whole kernel corn, cooked
1 cup water	• Salt and pepper to taste
1 tablespoon beef base or instant beef bouillon	2 to 3 pounds potatoes, cooked, mashed
1/2 cup honey, or to taste	
8 ounces fresh or frozen sliced carrots, cooked	

Melt 2 tablespoons butter in a large saucepan or Dutch oven. Add the onion. Sauté for 3 to 4 minutes or until transparent. Add the ground beef. Cook until the ground beef is brown and crumbly, stirring constantly. Sprinkle with flour and curry powder. Cook for 4 to 5 minutes, stirring constantly. Add the water, beef base and honey. Cook until thickened, stirring constantly. Add the carrots, green beans, green peas and corn and mix well. Season with salt and pepper. Spoon into an ovenproof baking dish, filling 2/3 full. Top with the mashed potatoes. Bake at 350 degrees for 1 hour or until heated through.

Note: May substitute onion or garlic jelly for the honey.

Meat Loaf with Worcestershire Baked Potatoes

Yield: 12 servings

2	pounds ground beef	1	teaspoon salt
1	pound bulk pork sausage	1	teaspoon (heaping) freshly cracked pepper
1	whole head garlic, chopped		
2	medium onions, chopped	2	eggs, lightly beaten
1	small or medium green bell pepper	•	Thickly sliced bacon
1	small or medium red bell pepper	•	Basting Sauce (page 127)
1	cup cornflakes, crushed	•	Worcestershire Baked Potatoes (page 127)
1	tablespoon (heaping) sweet pickle relish		

Crumble the ground beef and sausage into a large bowl. Add the garlic, onions and bell peppers and mix well. Stir in the cornflakes, pickle relish, salt and pepper. Add the eggs. Knead by hand just until mixed. Shape into a 4 1/2-inch wide by 4 1/2-inch deep loaf in a baking pan. Wrap the loaf with bacon. Bake at 350 degrees for 45 minutes.

Brush the top and sides with Basting Sauce. Turn the loaf over. Brush with Basting Sauce. Bake for 45 minutes longer or until cooked through. Brush with additional Basting Sauce. Remove the meat loaf to a large serving dish. Arrange the Worcestershire Baked Potatoes around the meat loaf. Serve immediately with a tossed green salad and a good beer.

Note: The density of the meat loaf depends on how firmly you knead it. Some prefer a rather loose, but thorough, mix.

Basting Sauce

5 or 6 garlic cloves, chopped
1 small onion, chopped
1/4 cup (1/2 stick) butter
1 cup catsup

1 tablespoon liquid smoke
1/4 cup (or more) packed dark
brown sugar

Sauté the garlic and onion in the butter in a small saucepan until tender. Stir in the catsup, liquid smoke and brown sugar. Cook over medium heat for 5 to 10 minutes, stirring occasionally; do not boil.

Worcestershire Baked Potatoes

12 baking potatoes
3 to 4 tablespoons Worcestershire
sauce

1/4 cup (1/2 stick) butter, melted
• Salt to taste

Rinse the unpeeled potatoes and pat dry. Let stand until completely dry. Coat the potatoes with some of the Worcestershire sauce. Arrange on a baking sheet. Bake at 350 degrees for 30 minutes. Coat with additional Worcestershire sauce. Bake for 30 minutes longer. Brush with the butter and sprinkle with salt. Bake for 5 to 10 minutes longer or until cooked through and brown and crusty on the outside.

Enticing Kabobs

Yield: 12 servings

1/3	cup olive oil		1	teaspoon oregano
1/4	cup vinegar		1	teaspoon celery salt
1/4	cup lemon juice		1	tablespoon parsley
1	garlic clove, minced		1	tablespoon rosemary
1	teaspoon salt		1	bay leaf
1/2	teaspoon pepper		5	pounds beef or lamb, cubed
1	teaspoon basil			

Combine the olive oil, vinegar, lemon juice, garlic, salt, pepper, basil, oregano, celery salt, parsley, rosemary and bay leaf in a large bowl and mix well. Add the beef and toss to coat well. Marinate, covered, in the refrigerator for 3 days, stirring daily.

Drain the beef, discarding the marinade. Thread the beef onto skewers. Grill over medium coals for 5 to 7 minutes or until cooked through.

Portland is closer to Europe than any other United States transatlantic port.

Rosemary-Crusted Rack of Lamb with Olive Oil-Smashed Potatoes

Yield: 4 servings

This is a popular favorite at the Back Bay Grill in Portland. Chef Larry Matthews, Jr. apprenticed at the White Barn Inn and now oversees another top-rated kitchen in his native Maine. His flavorful appetizer, Seared Maine Diver Scallops with Roasted Corn Salsa, appears on page 30 and his dessert accompaniment, Maine Blueberries with Grand Marnier Sabayon, appears on page 154.

2	lamb racks		2	cups veal demi-glace
•	Salt and pepper to taste		4	russet potatoes
•	Dijon mustard to taste		•	Extra-virgin olive oil to taste
2	bunches rosemary, finely chopped		1	bunch flat Italian parsley, chopped
1	bunch Swiss chard		1	bunch chives
1	cup port wine		1	bunch tarragon

Trim the lamb of all excess fat. Season with salt and pepper. Coat the lamb with Dijon mustard; pat with the rosemary until adheres to the lamb. Place on a rack in a roasting pan. Bake at 400 degrees for 20 minutes or until the lamb tests done.

Cut the ribs out of the Swiss chard and crosscut into 1/2-inch strips. Heat the port in a saucepan until reduced by 1/2. Combine the port and veal demi-glace in a bowl. Stir in the Swiss chard. Season the sauce with salt and pepper. Set aside.

Peel the potatoes and chop into bite-size pieces. Boil in water to cover until tender; drain.

Heat the olive oil in a skillet. Add the potatoes and parsley, chives and tarragon. Heat until light brown, stirring to smash the potatoes into smaller chunks.

Place the potatoes in the center of a large serving platter. Cut the lamb into chops and arrange around the potatoes. Spoon the sauce around the chops.

Lamb Pastitsio

Yield: 8 servings

1	small onion, finely chopped		2	tablespoons ($^1/4$ stick) butter
5	garlic cloves, finely minced		2	tablespoons flour
3	tablespoons olive oil		$1^1/2$	cups milk
1	pound lean ground lamb		$^1/4$	cup grated Parmesan cheese
$1^1/2$	cups tomato sauce		•	Freshly grated nutmeg
5	tablespoons minced fresh parsley		8	ounces ziti or favorite pasta
•	Pinch of ground cinnamon		2	eggs
$^1/2$	teaspoon rosemary		2	tablespoons ($^1/4$ stick) butter
•	Salt and freshly ground pepper to taste		1	cup shredded Swiss cheese

Sauté the onion and garlic in the olive oil in a large skillet until soft. Add the lamb. Cook until browned, stirring constantly; drain. Add the tomato sauce, parsley, cinnamon, rosemary, salt and pepper. Set aside.

Melt 2 tablespoons butter in a heavy saucepan over medium heat. Blend in the flour with a wire whisk to form a roux. Add the milk gradually, stirring constantly. Cook until thickened, stirring constantly. Stir in the Parmesan cheese and nutmeg. Remove from the heat.

Cook the pasta in boiling salted water in a large saucepan for 10 minutes or until al dente; drain and return to the saucepan. Add the eggs and 2 tablespoons butter and mix well.

Place $^1/2$ of the pasta in a greased 9x13-inch baking pan. Cover with the lamb mixture. Sprinkle with $^1/2$ of the Swiss cheese. Layer the remaining pasta over the Swiss cheese. Pour the cream sauce over the layers. Sprinkle with the remaining Swiss cheese and nutmeg.

Bake at 375 degrees for 1 hour or until the top is puffy and golden brown.

Note: May prepare this recipe ahead of time and chill for 48 hours before baking. May also freeze this dish.

Greek Lamb and Spinach Pie

Yield: 12 servings

1	pound ground lamb	3	eggs
1	onion, chopped	8	ounces feta cheese, crumbled
1/4	cup (1/2 stick) butter	8	ounces grated Parmesan cheese
1	bunch scallions, sliced	1/2	cup (1 stick) butter
2	tablespoons dill	1	(16-ounce) package phyllo
1 1/2	tablespoons parsley flakes		
2	(10-ounce) packages frozen chopped spinach, thawed, drained		

Brown the ground lamb in a skillet, stirring until crumbly.

Sauté the onion in 1/4 cup butter in a large skillet until transparent. Add the scallions, dill and parsley flakes. Cook for 5 minutes. Add the spinach and mix well. Remove from the heat. Stir in the ground lamb.

Beat the eggs in a large bowl. Add the feta cheese and Parmesan cheese and mix until smooth. Add the spinach mixture and mix well.

Melt 1/2 cup butter in a saucepan. Brush an 11x14-inch baking dish with some of the melted butter. Cover the bottom of the dish with 2 layers phyllo dough; brush with melted butter. Repeat 4 times. Spread the spinach mixture over the phyllo dough layers. Cover with 4 more layers of phyllo dough brushed with butter. Pour remaining melted butter over the top. Bake at 400 degrees for 30 minutes.

Lamb and Carrot Meatballs

Yield: 6 servings

1	pound lean ground lamb	1/2	teaspoon pepper
2	cups shredded carrots	1/2	teaspoon basil
1	medium onion, chopped	2	tablespoons cornstarch
1	egg	1 1/2	cups fat-free bouillon
1	teaspoon salt		

Combine the ground lamb, carrots, onion, egg, salt, pepper and basil in a bowl and mix well. Shape by tablespoonfuls into balls. Brown the meatballs in a large skillet sprayed with nonstick canola cooking spray. Place the meatballs in a 2-quart baking dish, reserving the pan drippings.

Dissolve the cornstarch in the bouillon in a small bowl. Add to the reserved pan drippings in the skillet. Cook until thickened, stirring constantly. Pour over the meatballs. Bake, covered, at 350 degrees for 30 to 40 minutes or until the meatballs are cooked through.

Braised Lamb Chop Stew

Yield: 4 servings

4	arm lamb chops	1	(10-ounce) can chicken broth
1	teaspoon crushed fresh rosemary leaves	3	cups sliced vegetables, such as carrots, celery and onions
2	tablespoons soy sauce	•	Salt and pepper to taste

Brown the lamb chops in a small amount of vegetable oil in a Dutch oven. Season with the rosemary and soy sauce. Add the chicken broth. Bring to a boil. Add the vegetables and reduce the heat. Simmer for 30 minutes or until tender. Adjust the seasonings to taste.

Pork Tenderloin with Herb Crumb Crust

Yield: 4 servings

3 cups bread crumbs
1/3 cup chopped fresh parsley
1 tablespoon chopped fresh rosemary
3/4 teaspoon crumbled bay leaves

• Salt and pepper to taste
1 1/2 pounds pork tenderloin, trimmed
1 egg, beaten
2 tablespoons (1/4 stick) butter
1 tablespoon olive oil

Mix the bread crumbs, parsley, rosemary and bay leaves in a large bowl. Season with salt and pepper.

Sprinkle the pork with salt and pepper. Dip into the egg; roll in the bread crumb mixture coating completely.

Melt the butter in the olive oil in a large heavy skillet over medium heat. Add the pork. Cook for 5 to 10 minutes or until golden brown on all sides. Place on a rack in a roasting pan.

Bake at 375 degrees for 20 minutes or until a meat thermometer registers 155 degrees when inserted into the center of the pork and the crust is golden brown. Remove the pork to a cutting board. Let stand for 5 minutes. Season with salt and pepper. Cut the pork into slices and serve.

Sweet and Sauerkraut

Yield: 6 to 8 servings

1	pound kielbasa sausage	1¹/₂	cups maple syrup
2	medium onions	³/₄	cup gin
1	tablespoon butter		
2	pounds deli sauerkraut, rinsed, drained		

Cut the kielbasa and onions into ¹/₄-inch slices. Brown the kielbasa on both sides in a cast-iron skillet. Remove the kielbasa to a warm plate.

Melt the butter in the skillet. Add the onions. Cook until the onions are brown. Add the kielbasa and sauerkraut. Add ¹/₂ of the maple syrup and ¹/₂ of the gin and mix well. Simmer until the liquid is absorbed, stirring occasionally. Add the remaining maple syrup and gin. Simmer over low heat or in a slow cooker on Low for 1 hour or until the sauerkraut is golden.

Chicken with Sauerkraut

Yield: 4 servings

4	boneless skinless chicken breasts, pounded thin	1	(16-ounce) package sauerkraut, rinsed, drained
1	(8-ounce) bottle Russian salad dressing	4	ounces Swiss cheese, sliced

Place the chicken in a 9x13-inch glass baking dish. Pour the salad dressing over the chicken to cover. Spread the sauerkraut over the top. Bake at 375 degrees for 20 minutes. Layer the Swiss cheese over the chicken. Bake for 5 minutes longer or until the Swiss cheese melts.

Chicken San Juan

Yield: 6 to 8 servings

1	pound hot Italian sausage	2	cups coarsely chopped onions
2	(2¹/2-pound) chickens, cut up	1	tablespoon chopped garlic
•	Salt and pepper to taste	3	cups chopped tomatoes
1¹/2	pounds eggplant, cut into 1-inch pieces	1	cup uncooked rice
1	cup 1-inch pieces green bell pepper	2	cups chicken broth

Cook the sausage in a Dutch oven for 15 minutes or until brown. Remove the sausage with a slotted spoon to a warm platter. Add the chicken to the pan drippings in the Dutch oven. Cook for 10 minutes or until the chicken is brown. Season with salt and pepper. Remove the chicken to a warm platter.

Add the eggplant, green pepper, onions and garlic to the pan drippings in the Dutch oven. Cook for 10 minutes or until the vegetables are slightly wilted, stirring occasionally. Return the sausage and chicken to the Dutch oven. Add the tomatoes, uncooked rice and chicken broth. Cover and bring to a boil. Place the Dutch oven in the oven. Bake at 400 degrees for 40 minutes or until the chicken is cooked through.

Country Captain

Yield: 6 servings

Legend says this recipe came to Savannah via a captain who shared this recipe with his Georgia friends.

1 (3- to 3 1/2-pound) chicken, skinned, cut up	1 1/2 teaspoons salt
1/4 cup flour	1/2 teaspoon white pepper
1/2 teaspoon salt	1 1/2 teaspoons curry powder
1/8 teaspoon white pepper	1/2 teaspoon thyme
3 to 4 tablespoons vegetable oil	1/2 teaspoon chopped fresh parsley
2 onions, chopped (1 cup)	5 cups undrained canned tomatoes
2 green bell peppers, chopped (1 1/2 cups)	2 cups hot cooked rice
	1/4 cup currants
1 garlic clove, crushed	4 ounces blanched almonds, roasted

Coat the chicken with a mixture of flour, 1/2 teaspoon salt and 1/8 teaspoon white pepper. Brown the chicken in the vegetable oil in a large heavy skillet. Remove the chicken to a platter and keep warm.

Add the onions, green peppers and garlic to the drippings in the skillet. Cook until the onions are light brown, stirring constantly. Add 1 1/2 teaspoons salt, 1/2 teaspoon white pepper, curry powder, thyme, parsley and tomatoes and mix well.

Arrange the chicken in a shallow roasting pan. Pour the tomato mixture over the chicken, adding water if the mixture doesn't cover the chicken. Bake, covered, at 350 degrees for 45 minutes or until the chicken is tender and cooked through.

To serve, arrange the chicken in the center of a large platter, reserving the sauce. Spoon the hot rice around the chicken. Stir the currants into the reserved sauce. Pour over the rice. Sprinkle with the almonds. Garnish with fresh parsley.

Firecracker Chicken

Yield: 10 servings

1	cup salted roasted peanuts	2	tablespoons chopped fresh
1	(10-ounce) jar orange marmalade		tarragon
1/2	cup olive oil	2	teaspoons curry powder
1/2	cup orange juice	1	teaspoon salt
3	tablespoons Dijon mustard	18	to 22 chicken pieces

Process the peanuts in a food processor until finely ground. Combine the ground peanuts, orange marmalade, olive oil, orange juice, Dijon mustard, tarragon, curry powder and salt in a bowl and mix well.

Arrange the chicken in two 9x13-inch baking pans. Pour the marinade over the chicken. Marinate, covered, in the refrigerator for 6 to 12 hours, turning occasionally.

Drain the marinade from the chicken into a saucepan. Boil the marinade for 2 to 3 minutes.

Bake the chicken at 350 degrees for 20 to 35 minutes or until the chicken is partially cooked. Place the chicken on a grill rack. Grill for 10 minutes on each side or until the chicken is cooked through, basting with the cooked marinade as needed.

Yogurt Chicken

Yield: 6 servings

3	skinless chicken breasts	2	tablespoons Dijon mustard
2	tablespoons lemon juice	1/4	teaspoon Worcestershire sauce
•	Cayenne pepper and/or Tabasco sauce to taste	1/2	teaspoon thyme leaves
		1/4	cup minced green onions
1	cup low-fat or fat-free plain yogurt	•	Paprika to taste
2	tablespoons flour	2	tablespoons grated Parmesan cheese
1/4	cup low-fat or fat-free mayonnaise		

Arrange the chicken in a lightly oiled 8x8-inch baking dish. Drizzle with the lemon juice. Sprinkle with cayenne pepper and/or Tabasco sauce.

Mix the yogurt with the flour in a small bowl. Add the mayonnaise, Dijon mustard, Worcestershire sauce and thyme and mix well. Spread over the chicken. Sprinkle with green onions and paprika.

Bake, uncovered, at 350 degrees for 45 minutes. Sprinkle the chicken evenly with Parmesan cheese. Broil 6 inches from the heat source until the Parmesan cheese is light brown.

Note: The recipe can easily be doubled and baked in a 10x13-inch baking dish.

Sesame Chicken

Yield: 4 to 6 servings

1	package plain croutons	2	pounds boneless skinless
3/4	cup sesame seeds, toasted		chicken breasts
1	tablespoon paprika	•	Flour
2	teaspoons garlic powder	•	Vegetable oil for frying
1 1/2	teaspoons salt	1	(10-ounce) jar apricot preserves
3/4	teaspoon freshly ground pepper	2	teaspoons soy sauce
2	eggs	1/4	cup water
2	tablespoons soy sauce	•	Garlic salt to taste
2	tablespoons water		

Process the croutons in a blender until fine crumbs form. Combine the processed crumbs, sesame seeds, paprika, garlic powder, salt and pepper in a bowl and mix well.

Beat the eggs with 2 tablespoons soy sauce and 2 tablespoons water in a small bowl. Roll the chicken in enough flour to coat. Roll the chicken in the egg mixture; roll in the crumb mixture until coated. Fry in hot vegetable oil in a skillet until brown and cooked through. Drain on paper towels and keep warm.

Combine the preserves, 2 teaspoons soy sauce and 1/4 cup water in a bowl and mix well. Sprinkle with garlic salt.

To serve, dip the chicken in the preserve mixture or cover the chicken with the preserve mixture before serving.

Moutarde Chicken with Mushroom Sauce

Yield: 8 to 12 servings

The marinade for this recipe was originally intended as a salad dressing. When too much mustard was mistakenly added once, the idea arose to use it as a marinade for chicken. It worked! The marinade flavors mellow wonderfully as the chicken bakes.

8	to 12 boneless skinless chicken breasts	2	cups canola oil, or 1 cup vegetable oil and 1 cup olive oil
1	cup Dijon mustard	16	ounces fresh mushrooms
1	cup whole-grain mustard	1	tablespoon vegetable oil
1/2	cup lemon juice		

Cut each chicken breast into halves or thirds, trimming any excess skin or fat. Pound the chicken between plastic wrap with a meat mallet.

Combine the Dijon mustard, whole-grain mustard and lemon juice in a food processor container. Process until well blended. Add the canola oil gradually, processing constantly and adding additional mustard or lemon juice if desired to suit taste.

Place the chicken in a large covered container. Spoon the mustard mixture over the chicken. Marinate, covered, in the refrigerator for 10 to 12 hours.

Arrange the chicken in a single layer on a baking sheet, reserving the remaining marinade for the Mushroom Sauce. Bake at 350 degrees for 20 to 30 minutes or until cooked through.

For the Mushroom Sauce, sauté the mushrooms in the vegetable oil in a skillet until tender. Add the reserved marinade and mix well. Bring to a boil. Boil for 5 minutes, stirring constantly.

Remove the chicken to a serving dish. Spoon the Mushroom Sauce over the chicken. Garnish with thin slices of lemon. Serve with rice, a green vegetable, crusty bread and red or white wine.

May prepare the chicken and Mushroom Sauce 1 day in advance. Place in an ovenproof serving dish and chill, covered, until ready to serve. Bake at 350 degrees just until heated through. Garnish and serve.

Note: Try using the mustard marinade on chicken tenders to make a great hors d'oeuvre.

Lobster-Cooking Essentials

Use two quarts of clean seawater for each lobster, or use fresh tap water and add $1/2$ teaspoon salt per quart. The number of lobsters that are being prepared determines the size of kettle used. The water must fill the pot $1/2$ to not more than $2/3$ full. Bring water to a rolling boil over high heat. Place lobsters head first into the pot, completely submerging them.

Cover the pot tightly and quickly return to a boil. When water boils, begin timing. Regulate the heat to prevent water from boiling over, but be sure to keep the liquid boiling throughout cooking time.

Cooking time for a one- to two-pound hard-shell lobster is ten minutes per pound. Add three additional minutes per pound for each additional pound thereafter. For example, a two-pound lobster will cook for 13 minutes and a $1^1/2$-pound lobster will cook for $11^1/2$ minutes. If cooking soft-shell lobsters, reduce boiling time by three minutes.

The shells may turn red before the water even returns to a boil, so do not use color as an indication for doneness. The antenna pulls out easily when the lobster is done. Serve with melted butter and lemon wedges.

Chicken Florentine

Serves 6 to 8

This versatile dish can be served for brunch, lunch, or dinner. It can
be doubled or tripled easily.

6	to 8 boneless skinless chicken breasts	4	garlic cloves, chopped
•	Flour	1/4	cup (1/2 stick) butter
2	tablespoons canola or vegetable oil	1	cup dry white wine
10	ounces fresh spinach, rinsed, drained	1	to 2 teaspoons Dijon mustard
3	shallots, chopped	1	teaspoon instant chicken bouillon
		2	cups heavy cream
		•	Salt and pepper to taste

Trim any excess skin or fat from the chicken. Pound the chicken between plastic wrap with a meat mallet. Coat the chicken with flour. Cook in the canola oil in a skillet over medium-high heat until brown on both sides and cooked through.

Tear the spinach into very small pieces, discarding the stems and center veins. Sauté the shallots and garlic in the butter in a large skillet over medium heat until tender. Add the wine gradually, stirring constantly. Cook until the mixture is slightly reduced, stirring constantly. Add the spinach. Cook for 5 minutes, stirring frequently. Stir in the Dijon mustard and instant bouillon. Cook for 2 minutes longer, stirring constantly. Stir in the heavy cream. Season with salt and pepper. Add the chicken.

Simmer just until the sauce thickens and the chicken is heated through, stirring frequently. Serve immediately or reduce heat and keep warm until serving time. May keep warm in the oven. May prepare the chicken and/or sauce the day before and reheat. Serve with pasta or rice.

Note: For an elegant addition to a buffet, chop the chicken before adding to the sauce and use the sauce as a filling for puff pastry shells.

Chicken à la Genovese

Yield: 6 to 8 servings

This recipe is a perennial favorite from the first Portland Symphony Orchestra cookbook. Serve with a tossed salad, vegetable of choice and a white wine.

6 to 8 boneless skinless chicken breasts
$1/2$ cup flour
$1/2$ teaspoon salt
$1/2$ teaspoon pepper
$1/2$ teaspoon nutmeg
$3/4$ cup unsaturated oil
8 ounces Italian fontina cheese

1 cup heavy cream
8 ounces mushrooms, cut into halves
$1/4$ cup ($1/2$ stick) butter
8 ounces baked ham, cut into strips
1 tomato, sliced
$1/2$ cup freshly grated Parmesan cheese

Pound the chicken breasts with a heavy mallet between 2 sheets of foil until $1/4$ inch thick. Coat the chicken with a mixture of flour, salt, pepper and nutmeg. Fry in heated oil in a skillet for 10 to 15 minutes on each side or until brown. Arrange in a large shallow baking dish.

Melt the fontina cheese in the cream in a saucepan over low heat.

Sauté the mushrooms in the butter in a skillet until soft. Sprinkle over the chicken. Arrange the ham over the mushrooms. Pour the cheese mixture over the layers. Arrange the tomato slices in a circle on top. Sprinkle with Parmesan cheese. Bake at 350 degrees for 35 minutes or until bubbly and the Parmesan cheese turns brown.

Grilled Chicken Kabobs

Yield: 6 servings

6	boneless skinless chicken breasts	2	teaspoons thyme
1/2	cup olive oil	1	teaspoon salt
1/2	cup fresh lemon juice	1/4	teaspoon freshly ground pepper
2	tablespoons oregano		

Cut the chicken into 1-inch pieces. Place in a glass bowl. Combine the olive oil, lemon juice, oregano, thyme, salt and pepper in a bowl and mix well. Pour over the chicken and toss to coat. Marinate, covered, in the refrigerator for 24 hours.

Drain the chicken, discarding the marinade. Place the chicken on 6 skewers. Grill for 10 to 15 minutes or until the chicken is cooked through.

Lobster traps are rectangular in shape and are constructed of vinyl-coated wire. Herring is usually the bait of choice. The lobster is drawn toward the bait through a tunnel of netting that ends in a metal ring just in front of the bait. Once the lobster passes through the ring, it cannot exit. In Maine, by law, a lobster must measure between 3 1/4 inches and 5 inches long, or it must be returned to the sea. Lobster harvesters will also notch female, egg-bearing lobster (called V-notching) and throw them back to produce eggs for another year or two. These management and conservation techniques are a long-standing part of the lobstering tradition in Maine.

Vegetable Lasagna

Yield: 8 to 12 servings

1	(10-ounce) package spinach	16	ounces ricotta cheese
2	tablespoons (¹/₄ stick) butter	1	cup grated Parmesan or Romano
1	large onion, chopped		cheese
2	large green bell peppers, chopped	•	Basic Medium White Sauce
3	or 4 garlic cloves, finely chopped	16	ounces lasagna noodles, cooked,
8	ounces carrots, grated		drained
8	ounces mushrooms, chopped	3	cups shredded mozzarella cheese
4	eggs		

Tear the spinach leaves from the stems and center veins; rinse and pat dry. Chop finely.

Melt the butter in a large skillet. Add the onion. Sauté until translucent. Add the green peppers, garlic and carrots. Sauté for 5 to 10 minutes. Add the mushrooms and spinach. Sauté until tender. Increase the heat. Simmer until the liquid is reduced. Remove from the heat to cool.

Beat the eggs in a mixer bowl. Add the ricotta cheese and Parmesan cheese and beat well. Add the cooled vegetable mixture and blend well.

Pour enough Basic Medium White Sauce into a buttered 9x13-inch baking pan to coat the bottom. Alternate layers of noodles, vegetable and cheese mixture, noodles, Basic Medium White Sauce and shredded mozzarella cheese until the pan is full and always ending with a layer of sauce and mozzarella cheese. Bake, uncovered, at 350 degrees for 1 hour or until set. Let stand for 20 minutes before serving.

Note: Cover with a piece of foil if the top browns too fast during baking.

Basic Medium White Sauce

¹/₂	cup (1 stick) butter	4	cups milk
¹/₂	cup flour	•	Salt and pepper to taste

Melt the butter in a saucepan over low heat. Add the flour and blend well. Cook until the mixture bubbles, stirring occasionally. Add the milk gradually, whisking constantly with a wire whisk. Cook over medium heat until thickened, stirring constantly. Cook for 5 minutes, stirring constantly. Remove from the heat. Season with salt and pepper to taste.

Enchiladas Rojas

Yield: 5 servings

10	to 12 dried ancho chiles	1	to 1½ pounds mild cheese, such
1	ounce Abuelita chocolate		as Manchego or Monterey Jack
2	garlic cloves		cheese, shredded
1	teaspoon baking cocoa	•	Cream or sour cream
½	stick cinnamon	•	Chopped onion
•	Corn or vegetable oil	•	Shredded Iceberg lettuce
24	ounces corn tortillas		

Rinse and remove the seeds from the chiles. Boil the chiles in water to cover until soft; drain.

Process the chiles, chocolate, garlic, baking cocoa and cinnamon in a blender until smooth. Add enough water to make of a thick gravy consistency. Strain the mixture. Fry the mixture in corn oil in a skillet. Remove from the heat.

Fry the tortillas in oil in a skillet for a few seconds on each side. Place the tortillas in the chile mixture, turning to coat both sides. Place the cheese on the tortillas and roll up. Place in a baking dish. Pour any remaining chile mixture over the top. Bake at 300 degrees for 8 minutes. Serve with chopped onion, shredded lettuce and cream or sour cream.

Note: May prepare this recipe with chicken.

Standing Ovation

Desserts

Standing Ovation

Desserts

Blueberry Cake with Creamy Sauce

Yield: 6 to 9 servings

1¹/₂	cups sugar	1	teaspoon salt
¹/₂	cup shortening	¹/₂	cup buttermilk
2	eggs	1	teaspoon vanilla extract
2¹/₂	cups flour	2	cups blueberries
¹/₂	teaspoon baking soda	•	Creamy Sauce

Cream the sugar and shortening in a mixer bowl until light and fluffy. Beat in the eggs 1 at a time.

Mix the flour, baking soda and salt in a bowl. Add to the creamed mixture alternately with a mixture of the buttermilk and vanilla, beating just until mixed after each addition. Stir in the blueberries. Pour into a greased 9-inch square cake pan.

Bake at 350 degrees for 1 hour and 10 minutes or until cake tests done. May bake in a 9x13-inch cake pan and reduce baking time. Serve warm topped with Creamy Sauce.

Creamy Sauce

6	tablespoons (³/₄ stick) butter	1¹/₂	teaspoons vanilla extract
1¹/₂ to 1³/₄	cups confectioners' sugar	¹/₈	teaspoon salt
3	tablespoons warm milk		

Beat the butter in a mixer bowl until light and fluffy. Add the confectioners' sugar gradually, beating well after each addition. Beat in the milk gradually. Add the vanilla 1 drop at a time, beating constantly. Stir in the salt.

Wild Blueberries

The low-bush wild blueberry, *vaccinium angustifolium*, is one of only three native North American berries. It thrives in glacial soils and northern climates. The "barrens" of Maine, rolling plains of sandy soil, are considered optimum for growing blueberries, and today the state is responsible for more than 90 percent of the United States' blueberry production. From over 200,000 acres of barrens, primarily in Washington County, the annual yield is approximately thirty million pounds.

The barrens are stark, almost surreal, in appearance, with a smooth sea of blueberry plants broken only by an occasional glacial boulder or pine tree. In June, white blossoms dot the landscape, and the air is filled with the fragrance of ripening berries. The harvest occurs in August, with local families, Micmac Indians from New Brunswick, and other seasonal workers raking berries. Wild blueberries are often harvested in the traditional method, with handheld berry rakes that were invented in the 1880s by a local Mainer, Abijah Tabutt. Rakers perform a rapid push-and-twist motion with their wrists to separate the berries from the vine without crushing the fruit. Because of the hilly and rocky terrain in which the blueberry plant grows, mechanical harvesting cannot completely replace hand raking.

The demand for wild blueberries has been steadily increasing as research continues to show strong health and nutrition benefits related to eating blueberries. Because the blueberry is rated highest among fruits and vegetables for its antioxidant properties—that is, its ability to neutralize the free radicals associated with cancer, heart disease, and age-related health risks—it has been called a "Super Food."

Blueberry Gingerbread

Yield: 12 servings

1	cup sugar	1	teaspoon cinnamon
1/2	cup vegetable oil	1/2	teaspoon ginger
3	tablespoons molasses	1/2	teaspoon nutmeg
1/2	teaspoon salt	1	cup fresh or thawed frozen
1	egg		blueberries
2	cups flour	1	cup buttermilk
1	teaspoon baking soda	2	tablespoons sugar

Beat 1 cup sugar, vegetable oil, molasses and salt in a mixer bowl until well mixed. Add the egg and mix well.

Mix the flour, baking soda, cinnamon, ginger and nutmeg together. Coat the blueberries with some of the flour mixture.

Add the remaining flour mixture alternately with the buttermilk to the sugar mixture, beating well after each addition.

Stir in the blueberries. Pour into a greased and floured 7x15-inch baking dish. Sprinkle with 2 tablespoons sugar.

Bake at 350 degrees for 35 to 40 minutes or until a wooden pick inserted near the center comes out clean.

Cool in the dish for 10 minutes. Cut into squares. Serve warm with butter or whipped cream.

Blueberry Hermits

Yield: 6 to 8 dozen cookies

Stored in metal tins and packed in travel trunks, the earliest version of hermits can be traced back to Cape Cod, when sea travel was done aboard great clipper ships. The cookies contained valuable spices brought back by sailors from the Indies. Traditional hermits are made with dried fruit. This "Maine" version is a "fresh" idea of an old favorite.

2	cups packed brown sugar		1	teaspoon baking soda
1	cup shortening		1	teaspoon salt
2	eggs		1	teaspoon nutmeg
$1/2$	cup cold strong brewed coffee		1	teaspoon cinnamon
1	teaspoon vanilla extract		2	cups fresh blueberries
$3^1/2$	cups flour		1	cup sliced or chopped almonds

Cream the brown sugar and shortening in a bowl until light and fluffy. Add the eggs 1 at a time, mixing well after each addition. Beat in the coffee and vanilla.

Mix the flour, baking soda, salt, nutmeg and cinnamon in a bowl. Add to the creamed mixture gradually, mixing well after each addition. Fold in the blueberries and almonds.

Drop by rounded teaspoonfuls 2 inches apart onto a lightly greased cookie sheet. Bake at 375 degrees for 10 to 12 minutes or until the centers are firm when lightly touched.

Note: If using a dark or nonstick cookie sheet, decrease oven temperature to 350 degrees and bake for 8 to 10 minutes.

Independence Day Blueberry Pie

Yield: 6 to 8 servings

2	cups flour	1/2	cup sugar
2	teaspoons sugar	3	tablespoons flour
1	teaspoon salt	1/4	teaspoon cinnamon
2/3	cup shortening, chilled	1/8	teaspoon salt
3	to 4 tablespoons water	1 1/2	tablespoons fresh lemon juice
4	cups fresh Maine blueberries	1	tablespoon butter, chilled

Sift 2 cups flour, 2 teaspoons sugar and 1 teaspoon salt together into a bowl. Cut in the shortening until crumbly. Add the water 1 tablespoon at a time, mixing with a fork until the mixture forms a ball.

Chill, covered in plastic wrap, for 30 minutes or longer. Divide the pastry into 2 equal portions. Roll each portion into a 12-inch circle on a lightly floured surface. Fit 1 portion into a 9-inch pie plate.

Arrange the blueberries in the pie shell. Combine 1/2 cup sugar, 3 tablespoons flour, cinnamon and 1/8 teaspoon salt in a bowl and mix well. Sprinkle the sugar mixture and lemon juice over the blueberries. Dot with the butter.

Top with the remaining pastry, fluting the edge and cutting vents, or cut the remaining pastry into strips and arrange lattice-fashion over the pie. Cover the edge of the pie shell with foil to prevent excess browning.

Bake at 450 degrees for 10 minutes. Reduce oven temperature to 350 degrees. Bake for 30 to 40 minutes or until golden brown.

Blueberry Glacé Pie

Yield: 6 to 8 servings

4	cups small Maine blueberries	3	tablespoons cornstarch
1	cup water	1	baked (9-inch) pie shell
1	cup sugar	•	Whipped cream

Combine 1 cup of the blueberries and 2/3 cup of the water in a 2-quart saucepan over medium-high heat. Bring to a boil.

Mix the sugar, remaining 1/3 cup water and cornstarch in a bowl. Add to the blueberry mixture and mix well. Return to a boil, stirring constantly. Boil for 1 minute. Let stand to cool slightly.

Arrange 2 1/2 cups of the remaining blueberries in the pie shell, reserving the remaining blueberries for garnish.

Pour the cooked blueberry mixture over the blueberries in the pie shell. Let stand until cool. Garnish with whipped cream and reserved blueberries.

Maine Blueberries with Grand Marnier Sabayon

Yield: 12 to 16 servings

10	egg yolks	1	cup whipping cream
1	cup sugar	8	cups fresh blueberries
1/3	cup Grand Marnier	•	Confectioners' sugar

Combine the egg yolks, sugar and Grand Marnier in a double boiler. Whip for 8 to 10 minutes or until light and fluffy. Let stand to cool to room temperature.

Beat the whipping cream in a bowl until soft peaks form. Add to the egg yolk mixture and mix well.

Spoon equal portions of the blueberries into individual serving dishes. Top with some of the Grand Marnier Sabayon. Sprinkle with confectioners' sugar.

Note: See Editor's Note on page 58.

Blueberry Torte

Yield: 12 servings

This is a cheesecake-like torte—but without the fat!

1 1/2 cups flour
1/2 cup sugar
1 1/2 teaspoons baking powder
1/2 teaspoon cinnamon
1/4 teaspoon salt
1/4 cup canola oil
2 egg whites, lightly beaten
1 tablespoon butter, melted
1 teaspoon vanilla extract

1 large egg
2/3 cup fat-free sweetened condensed milk
2 tablespoons cornstarch
1 1/2 cups plain yogurt
• Zest of 1 lemon
1 teaspoon vanilla extract
3 cups fresh blueberries
• Confectioners' sugar

Spray a nonstick 9-inch round torte pan with nonstick baking spray.

Mix the flour, sugar, baking powder, cinnamon and salt in a bowl. Add the canola oil, egg whites, butter and 1 teaspoon vanilla and stir with a fork until well mixed. Press over the bottom of the prepared torte pan.

Whisk the egg, sweetened condensed milk and cornstarch in a bowl until smooth. Whisk in the yogurt until smooth. Blend in the lemon zest and 1 teaspoon vanilla. Pour over the prepared crust. Sprinkle the blueberries evenly over the top.

Bake at 300 degrees for 1 1/4 to 1 1/2 hours or just until the top is set. Cool in the pan on a wire rack. Loosen the edge of the torte with a knife; remove the outer ring of the torte pan. Dust the torte with confectioners' sugar. May serve warm or chilled.

Blueberry Peach Cobbler

Yield: 4 to 6 servings

1/4	cup sugar	1/2	cup sugar
1/4	cup packed brown sugar	1 1/2	teaspoons baking powder
1	tablespoon cornstarch	1/2	teaspoon salt
1/2	cup water	1/2	cup milk
2	cups sliced peaches	1/4	cup (1/2 stick) butter, softened
1	cup blueberries	2	tablespoons sugar
1	tablespoon lemon juice	1/4	teaspoon nutmeg
1	cup flour		

Mix 1/4 cup sugar, brown sugar, cornstarch and water in a saucepan. Cook over medium heat for 5 minutes or until thick, stirring constantly.

Add the peaches, blueberries and lemon juice, stirring to mix. Spoon into a buttered 2-quart baking dish.

Sift the flour, 1/2 cup sugar, baking powder and salt together into a mixer bowl. Beat in the milk and butter until smooth. Spoon evenly over the peach mixture. Sprinkle with a mixture of 2 tablespoons sugar and nutmeg.

Bake at 375 degrees for 40 to 45 minutes or until hot and bubbly. Serve with vanilla ice cream or freshly whipped cream flavored with a little sugar and vanilla.

Blueberry Snow with Mint

Yield: 2 servings

1/2 cup fresh or thawed frozen blueberries	2 tablespoons sugar
	1/3 cup whipping cream
1 tablespoon sugar	1/3 cup plain yogurt
1 egg white	1 tablespoon chopped fresh mint

Combine the blueberries and 1 tablespoon sugar in a small heavy saucepan. Cook over low heat until the sugar is dissolved and the blueberries are soft. Let stand to cool.

Whisk the egg white in a bowl until soft peaks form. Add 2 tablespoons sugar gradually, whisking constantly until stiff peaks form and egg white is smooth and glossy.

Beat the whipping cream in a mixer bowl just until thick. Stir in the yogurt. Add the whipped cream mixture, blueberry mixture and chopped mint alternately to the egg white mixture, folding just until mixture appears marbled.

Spoon into individual serving dishes. Garnish with mint.

Maine, with over eighty percent of its land covered by trees, is the most heavily forested state in the country. The pulp and paper industry in Maine generates two billion dollars a year.

Blueberry Melba

Yield: 8 servings

If you have help in the kitchen, this dessert can be made truly memorable by serving it in
tall parfait glasses. Prepare peaches as directed, but slice each half into bite-size pieces.
Use a small ice cream scoop and work quickly. Layer Melba Sauce, peaches, ice cream and
blueberries in each glass and repeat the layers until the glass is full. Present guests
with a long spoon and let them dig in.

1	to 2 quarts water	2	cups fresh blueberries
4	very ripe peaches	•	Melba Sauce
1	quart vanilla ice cream or frozen yogurt		

Bring the water to a boil in a large saucepan. Submerge peaches 1 at a time in the boiling water
for 1 minute. Remove from the water. Plunge into cold water. Peel with a small paring knife. Cut
into halves and remove the pit.

Place a peach half in each of 8 individual serving dishes. Add a generous scoop of the ice cream
and some of the blueberries. Top with the Melba Sauce. Garnish with a sprig of fresh mint.

Note: May use any leftover blueberries in pancakes and serve with a mixture of leftover Melba
Sauce and maple syrup, or mix all the remaining peaches, blueberries and Melba Sauce and serve
over Belgian waffles.

Melba Sauce

$1/2$	cup sugar	$1/2$	cup orange juice or water
2	tablespoons cornstarch	1	tablespoon lemon juice
1	(10-ounce) package frozen raspberries in syrup, thawed	$1/2$	teaspoon cinnamon

Mix the sugar and cornstarch in a heavy saucepan. Stir in the undrained raspberries, orange
juice, lemon juice and cinnamon. Bring to a boil over medium heat, stirring constantly. Cook
for 5 to 10 minutes or until thickened, stirring frequently to break up the raspberries. Let stand
to cool.

Blueberry Cream Pie

Yield: 6 to 8 servings

Why not combine the best of both worlds—cream pie and fresh blueberries?
This cool and sweet recipe is a great end to a hot summer evening.

1	cup sugar	2	tablespoons ($^1/_4$ stick) butter
$^1/_4$	cup cornstarch	2	teaspoons vanilla extract
$^1/_2$	teaspoon salt	2	cups fresh blueberries
$2^1/_2$	cups whole or low-fat milk	1	baked (9-inch) deep-dish pie shell
4	egg yolks	•	Meringue (optional)

Mix the sugar, cornstarch and salt in a heavy saucepan over medium heat. Add the milk gradually, stirring until well blended. Cook until thickened and bubbly, stirring constantly; do not allow mixture to come to a full boil. Cook for 2 minutes longer, stirring constantly. Remove from the heat.

Beat the egg yolks in a bowl until thick and pale yellow. Beat in about 1 cup of the hot mixture. Add the egg yolk mixture to the hot mixture and mix well. Cook over medium heat for 2 to 5 minutes or until very thick, stirring constantly. Remove from the heat. Stir in the butter and vanilla. Fold in the blueberries. Pour into the pie shell.

Spread the Meringue over the filling, sealing to the edge. Bake at 350 degrees for 12 to 15 minutes or until golden brown. Cool on a wire rack. Chill until ready to serve.

Note: May omit the meringue and top with sweetened whipped cream just before serving.

Meringue

4	egg whites, at room temperature	$^1/_2$	teaspoon vanilla extract
$^1/_2$	teaspoon cream of tartar	$^1/_2$	cup sugar

Beat the egg whites, cream of tartar and vanilla in a large mixer bowl until thick and foamy. Add the sugar 1 tablespoon at a time, beating constantly. Beat until stiff peaks form.

Apricot Nectar Cake

Yield: 12 servings

1	(2-layer) package lemon cake mix	1/2	cup vegetable oil
1/2	cup sugar	1 3/4	cups confectioners' sugar
4	eggs	1/4	cup lemon juice
1	cup apricot nectar		

Combine the cake mix and sugar in a large mixer bowl, stirring to mix. Add the eggs, apricot nectar and vegetableoil.

Beat at medium speed for 6 minutes. Pour into a greased and floured bundt pan.

Bake at 350 degrees for 45 minutes or until cake tests done. Cool in the pan for 10 minutes. Invert onto a cake plate.

Stir the confectioners' sugar and lemon juice together in a bowl. Drizzle over the warm cake.

Chocolate Chip Oatmeal Cake

Yield: 15 servings

1	cup quick-cooking oats	1 3/4	cups flour
1 3/4	cups boiling water	1	teaspoon baking soda
1	cup sugar	1/2	teaspoon salt
1	cup packed brown sugar	1	tablespoon baking cocoa
1/2	cup (1 stick) margarine, softened	2	cups chocolate chips
3	eggs	3/4	cup chopped walnuts

Mix the oats and boiling water in a mixer bowl. Let stand to cool for 10 minutes. Beat in the sugar, brown sugar, margarine and eggs. Stir in a mixture of the flour, baking soda, salt, baking cocoa and 1 cup of the chocolate chips. Spoon into a greased 9x13-inch baking pan. Top with the walnuts and remaining chocolate chips. Bake at 350 degrees for 35 to 40 minutes or until cake tests done. Let stand to cool for 10 minutes.

Date Chocolate Chip Cake

Yield: 16 servings

The dates in this "special-occasion" cake make it so moist and rich
that there's no need for frosting.

1 cup boiling water	1/2 cup (1 stick) butter
1 (16-ounce) package chopped dates	1 cup sugar
1 tablespoon baking soda	2 eggs
1 3/4 cups flour	1 teaspoon vanilla extract
1 tablespoon baking cocoa	1 cup chocolate chips
	1/2 cup chopped pecans

Pour boiling water over the dates in a bowl. Stir in the baking soda. Let stand for 10 minutes. Sift the flour and baking cocoa together.

Cream the butter and sugar in a mixer bowl until light and fluffy. Add the eggs 1 at a time, beating well after each addition. Add the undrained dates alternately with the flour mixture, beating constantly. Add the vanilla; beat for 2 minutes. Stir in 1/2 cup of the chocolate chips. Spoon into a greased and floured tube pan. Sprinkle with the pecans and remaining 1/2 cup chocolate chips.

Bake at 350 degrees for 45 to 60 minutes or until cake tests done. Cool in the pan for 10 minutes. Remove to a wire rack to cool completely.

Treasure Chest Cake

Yield: 12 servings

1	large orange	$^1/_4$	teaspoon cloves
1	cup walnuts	$^1/_4$	teaspoon allspice
1	cup baking raisins	$^1/_2$	cup shortening
2	cups flour	1	cup sugar
1	teaspoon baking powder	1	egg, beaten
$^3/_4$	teaspoon baking soda	1	teaspoon vanilla extract
$^1/_2$	teaspoon salt	1	cup buttermilk
$^1/_2$	teaspoon cinnamon	2	cups confectioners' sugar

Squeeze the juice from the orange. Remove the orange peel, discarding the membrane and white pithy layer. Grind the orange peel, walnuts and raisins coarsely. Combine with the orange juice in a bowl.

Sift the flour, baking powder, baking soda, salt, cinnamon, cloves and allspice together 3 times into a bowl.

Cream the shortening and sugar in a mixer bowl until light and fluffy. Beat in the egg and vanilla until light. Add the flour mixture alternately with the buttermilk, mixing well after each addition. Stir in all but $^3/_4$ cup of the orange mixture. Spoon into a 4x8-inch loaf pan.

Bake at 350 degrees for 50 minutes or until cake tests done. Cool in the pan for 10 minutes. Remove to a cake plate.

Mix the confectioners' sugar with the remaining orange mixture in a bowl, adding enough additional orange juice to make of desired consistency. Spread over the warm cake.

Note: Seeded Muscat grapes are even better than raisins in this recipe, but they are sometimes difficult to find.

Pistachio Pound Cake

Yield: 10 servings

1	(2-layer) package yellow cake mix	1/2	cup orange juice
1	(4-ounce) package instant pistachio pudding mix	4	eggs
		1	teaspoon vanilla extract
1/2	cup water	3/4	cup chocolate syrup

Stir the cake mix and pudding mix in a mixer bowl. Add the water, orange juice, eggs and vanilla and beat on medium speed for 2 minutes.

Spoon 3/4 of the batter into a greased and floured tube pan. Add the chocolate syrup to the remaining batter and mix well. Spoon over the batter in the tube pan.

Bake at 350 degrees for 1 hour. Cool in the pan for 10 minutes. Remove to a wire rack to cool completely.

As an illustrator of Civil War battlefields for Harper's Weekly, *the renowned artist Winslow Homer came to live at Prout's Neck.*

Bucksport Whoopie Pies

Yield: 12 to 15 servings

More Whoopie Pies are made in Maine than anyplace else in the United States, although the confection may not have originated in the state. The Pennsylvania Dutch reportedly invented this cake made like a cookie, but called a pie. Where did the name come from? Mainers like to think it was the enthusiastic reaction of kids upon their first bite.

2	cups flour		2	egg yolks
1	cup sugar		1	teaspoon vanilla extract
1	teaspoon baking powder		2	egg whites
1	teaspoon baking soda		1	teaspoon vanilla extract
1	teaspoon salt		1/2	cup shortening
5	tablespoons baking cocoa		1	(1-pound) package confectioners'
1	cup plus 2 tablespoons milk			sugar
1/2	cup shortening			

Mix the flour, sugar, baking powder, baking soda, salt and baking cocoa in a large mixer bowl. Beat in the milk, 1/2 cup shortening, egg yolks and 1 teaspoon vanilla. Drop by tablespoonfuls onto a greased baking sheet. Bake at 375 degrees for 8 to 10 minutes or until slightly crispy around the edges. Remove to waxed paper to cool.

Beat the egg whites in a medium mixer bowl just until foamy. Mix in 1 teaspoon vanilla and 1/2 cup shortening. Add the confectioners' sugar and beat until well mixed. Spread over 1/2 of the cooled Whoopie Pies. Top with the remaining Whoopie Pies.

Note: Wrap Whoopie Pies individually to prevent them from sticking to each other.

Cardamom Cookies

Yield: 2¹/₂ to 3 dozen cookies

1¹/₂	cups sugar	1	tablespoon ground cardamom
1	cup (2 sticks) margarine	2	teaspoons cinnamon
1	egg	1	teaspoon ginger
1	teaspoon molasses	1	teaspoon cloves
2¹/₂	cups flour	1	teaspoon nutmeg
1	teaspoon baking soda	1	teaspoon allspice
¹/₂	teaspoon salt		

Cream the sugar and margarine in a mixer bowl until light and fluffy. Beat in the egg and molasses. Mix the flour, baking soda, salt, cardamom, cinnamon, ginger, cloves, nutmeg and allspice in a bowl. Add to the creamed mixture and mix well. Chill, covered, for 1 to 2 hours.

Roll the dough very thin on a floured surface. Cut as desired. Arrange on a cookie sheet. Bake at 400 degrees for 8 to 10 minutes or just until brown. Cool on the cookie sheet for 2 minutes. Remove to a wire rack to cool completely.

Sebago Shortbread

Yield: 4 dozen cookies

4	cups sifted flour	2	cups (4 sticks) butter or
1	cup packed light brown sugar		margarine
1/2	teaspoon salt	1	teaspoon vanilla extract

Mix the flour, brown sugar and salt in a large bowl. Cut in the butter until the mixture is crumbly. Stir in the vanilla.

Pat 1/2 inch thick on a floured surface. Cut as desired. Arrange on a cookie sheet.

Bake at 325 degrees for 20 to 25 minutes or until light brown. Cool on the cookie sheet for 2 minutes. Remove to a wire rack to cool completely.

There are two kinds of foghorns found along the Maine coast, grunters and groaners.
A "groaner" has one long tone and a "grunter" is the two-toned version.

Molasses Sugar Cookies

Yield: 2 to 3 dozen cookies

3/4   cup shortening
1   cup sugar
1/4   cup molasses
1   egg
2   cups sifted flour
2   teaspoons baking soda

1/2   teaspoon salt
1   teaspoon cinnamon
1/2   teaspoon cloves
1/2   teaspoon ginger
•   Sugar

Melt the shortening in a 3- to 4-quart saucepan over low heat. Let stand to cool. Add 1 cup sugar, molasses and egg and beat well.

Sift the flour, baking soda, salt, cinnamon, cloves and ginger together. Stir into the shortening mixture. Chill, covered, for 1 to 2 hours or until firm.

Shape into 1-inch balls. Roll in sugar. Arrange 2 inches apart on a greased cookie sheet.

Bake at 375 degrees for 11 minutes or until golden brown. Cool on the cookie sheet for 2 minutes. Remove to a wire rack to cool completely.

Date Crumbles

Yield: 2 dozen squares

1¹/2 cups rolled oats	1/2 teaspoon salt
1¹/2 cups flour	1/2 cup crushed walnuts
1 cup packed brown sugar	3/4 cup (1¹/2 sticks) butter
1 teaspoon baking soda	• Date Filling

Mix the oats, flour, brown sugar, baking soda, salt and walnuts in a bowl. Cut in the butter until the mixture is crumbly.

Press 1/2 of the oat mixture over the bottom of a buttered 9x13-inch baking pan. Spread with the Date Filling. Crumble the remaining oat mixture over the top.

Bake at 350 degrees for 25 to 30 minutes or until hot and bubbly. Cool. Cut into squares.

Date Filling

1 (16-ounce) package chopped dates	1/2 cup sugar
1 cup boiling water	1 tablespoon flour
	1 teaspoon vanilla extract

Combine the dates, water, sugar, flour and vanilla in a double boiler. Cook until thickened, stirring frequently.

Chocolate Chip Oatmeal Bars

Yield: 2 dozen bars

1³/₄ cups flour	2 tablespoons milk
1 teaspoon baking soda	2 teaspoons vanilla extract
1 cup (2 sticks) butter, softened	2¹/₂ cups rolled oats
1¹/₄ cups packed brown sugar	2 cups semisweet chocolate chips
¹/₂ cup sugar	1 cup chopped pecans
2 eggs	

Combine the flour and baking soda and mix well. Beat the butter, brown sugar and sugar in a mixer bowl until creamy. Add the eggs, milk and vanilla and beat well. Add the flour mixture and mix well. Stir in the oats, chocolate chips and pecans. Press over the bottom of an ungreased 9x13-inch baking pan. Bake at 375 degrees for 30 minutes.

Kentucky Festival Pie

Yield: 8 servings

1 cup sugar	1 teaspoon vanilla extract
¹/₄ cup (¹/₂ stick) butter	¹/₂ cup chocolate chips
3 eggs, lightly beaten	¹/₂ cup pecans, chopped
³/₄ cup light corn syrup	3 tablespoons bourbon (optional)
¹/₄ teaspoon salt	1 unbaked (9-inch) pie shell

Cream the sugar and butter in a mixer bowl until light and fluffy. Beat in the eggs, corn syrup, salt and vanilla. Stir in the chocolate chips, pecans and bourbon. Spoon into the pie shell.

Bake at 375 degrees for 40 to 50 minutes. Let stand to cool. Serve with whipped cream or ice cream.

French Silk Pie

Yield: 6 to 8 servings

18	chocolate sandwich cookies	2/3	cup butter
1/4	cup Kahlúa	4	ounces unsweetened chocolate, melted
2	tablespoons (1/4 stick) butter, melted	1	teaspoon vanilla extract
1	cup sugar	3	extra-large eggs

Chop the cookies finely in a food processor. Combine the cookie crumbs with the Kahlúa and 2 tablespoons butter in a bowl, mixing until a ball forms. Press over the bottom and up the side of a 10-inch pie plate.

Beat the sugar and 2/3 cup butter in a mixer bowl until light and fluffy. Add the melted chocolate and vanilla and mix well, scraping the side of the bowl frequently. Beat in 1 of the eggs for 4 minutes. Add 1 of the remaining eggs and beat for 3 minutes. Beat in the remaining egg for 2 minutes.

Spoon into the prepared pie shell. Garnish with confectioners' sugar and/or grated chocolate. Chill, covered, until serving time.

Note: See Editor's Note on page 58.

Rich Fudge Pie

Yield: 6 to 8 servings

A chocolate lover's delight, this pie should be the consistency of a chewy brownie.

1/2	cup (1 stick) butter	2	eggs
2	ounces unsweetened chocolate	1	cup pecan halves
1	cup sugar	1	teaspoon vanilla extract

Melt the butter and chocolate in a double boiler, stirring to mix. Whisk in the sugar and eggs until fluffy. Add the pecans and vanilla and mix well. Pour into a buttered 9-inch pie plate. Bake at 325 degrees for 35 minutes. Serve with whipped cream or coffee ice cream.

Coconut Cream Pie

Yield: 10 servings

2	cups whipping cream	1	tablespoon unflavored gelatin
6	egg yolks	1/2	cup cold water
1	cup sugar	1	baked (10-inch) pie shell
1	teaspoon vanilla extract	1	cup flaked coconut, toasted

Beat the whipping cream in a mixer bowl until stiff peaks form. Whisk the egg yolks in a bowl. Add the sugar and vanilla, stirring to blend well. Soften the gelatin in the cold water in a saucepan. Bring to a boil, stirring to dissolve the gelatin. Stir a small amount of the hot mixture into the egg mixture; stir the egg mixture into the hot mixture. Let stand to cool. Fold into the whipped cream. Pour into the pie shell. Chill for 1 hour. Sprinkle the toasted coconut over the top just before serving.

Note: See *Editor's Note* on page 58.

Custard Meringue Pie

Yield: 6 to 8 servings

1¹/₃ cups crushed graham crackers	3 tablespoons cornstarch
6 tablespoons (³/₄ stick) butter, softened	1¹/₂ teaspoons vanilla extract
¹/₂ cup sugar	¹/₈ teaspoon salt
3 cups milk	4 egg whites, at room temperature
³/₄ cup sugar	6 tablespoons sugar
3 egg yolks	¹/₄ teaspoon salt
	¹/₂ teaspoon vanilla extract

Combine the graham cracker crumbs, butter and ¹/₂ cup sugar in a bowl and mix with a fork. Press over the bottom and up the side of a 9-inch pie plate. Bake at 375 degrees for 8 to 10 minutes. Let stand to cool.

Mix the milk, ³/₄ cup sugar, egg yolks, cornstarch, 1¹/₂ teaspoons vanilla and ¹/₈ teaspoon salt in a double boiler. Cook for 20 to 25 minutes or until thickened, stirring occasionally. Pour into the prepared pie shell.

Place the egg whites and 6 tablespoons sugar in a glass bowl in a pan of hot water, stirring until mixture is warm. Add ¹/₄ teaspoon salt and ¹/₂ teaspoon vanilla and mix well. Remove bowl from the water bath. Beat the egg white mixture until stiff peaks form. Spread over the pie filling, sealing to the edge. Bake at 300 degrees for 10 minutes or until the meringue is golden brown. Let stand to cool.

Zesty Orange Pie

Yield: 6 servings

1	cup sugar	•	Lemon juice to taste
3	tablespoons flour	•	Grated zest of 1 orange
2	eggs, beaten	1/8	teaspoon salt
1	cup orange juice	1	baked (9-inch) pie shell
1/2	cup water		

Mix the sugar and flour in a saucepan. Stir in the eggs, orange juice, water, lemon juice, orange zest and salt. Cook over medium heat for 5 to 8 minutes or until thickened, stirring often. Let stand to cool. Pour into the cooled pie shell. Serve with whipped cream.

Peak's Island Pear Pie

Yield: 6 to 8 servings

4	large ripe pears, peeled, thinly sliced	1/2	cup shredded Cheddar cheese
1/3	cup sugar	1/2	cup flour
1	tablespoon cornstarch	1/4	cup (1/2 stick) butter or margarine, melted
1/8	teaspoon salt	1/4	cup sugar
1	unbaked (9-inch) pie shell	1/4	teaspoon salt

Combine the pears, 1/3 cup sugar, cornstarch and 1/8 teaspoon salt in a bowl, tossing to coat the pears. Spoon into the pie shell. Combine the cheese, flour, butter, 1/4 cup sugar and 1/4 teaspoon salt in a bowl and mix until crumbly. Sprinkle over the pie filling. Bake at 425 degrees for 25 to 35 minutes or until the crust is golden brown and the cheese is melted. Cool on a wire rack for 10 minutes. Serve warm. Store, covered, in the refrigerator.

Apple Pan Dowdy

Yield: 4 to 6 servings

1	cup flour	•	Brown sugar to taste
1	cup sugar	•	Cinnamon to taste
1	teaspoon baking powder	2	tablespoons (1/4 stick) butter,
1	egg, beaten		melted
4	apples, peeled, sliced		

Sift the flour, sugar and baking powder together into a bowl. Add the egg, stirring until the mixture is crumbly. Place the apples in an 8-inch square baking pan. Sprinkle with a mixture of the brown sugar and cinnamon. Spoon the flour mixture over the top. Drizzle with the butter. Bake at 350 degrees for 35 minutes. Serve warm.

Espresso Crepes

Yield: 6 to 8 servings

1/3	cup sifted flour	2	eggs
2	teaspoons sugar	1 1/2	cups blueberries, raspberries
1/2	teaspoon cinnamon		and/or sliced strawberries
1/2	cup espresso or double-strength	1	cup sour cream
	coffee	2	tablespoons confectioners' sugar

Combine the flour, sugar and cinnamon in a bowl and mix well. Beat in a mixture of the espresso and eggs.

Heat a 6- or 7-inch crepe pan or heavy skillet over medium heat until drops of water sizzle and quickly evaporate. Brush the crepe pan lightly with melted butter or spray with oil. Pour 2 tablespoons of batter at a time into the crepe pan, tilting pan quickly to spread the batter. Cook each side for 1 or 2 minutes or until light brown. Remove crepe and keep warm.

Mix the berries and sour cream in a bowl. Spoon a small amount down the center of each crepe, folding to enclose the filling. Sprinkle each serving with a small amount of the confectioners' sugar. Garnish with additional berries.

Fresh Peach Cake Roll

Yield: 8 servings

1	cup flour	1	teaspoon vanilla extract
1	teaspoon baking powder	•	Confectioners' sugar
1/4	teaspoon salt	8	ounces cream cheese, softened
3	eggs	1	cup chopped fresh peaches
1	cup sugar	1/2	cup confectioners' sugar
1/3	cup water	1/8	teaspoon almond flavoring

Sift the flour, baking powder and salt together. Beat the eggs in a mixer bowl for 5 minutes. Add the sugar, water and vanilla gradually, beating constantly. Beat in the flour mixture. Pour the batter into a 10x15-inch jelly roll pan lined with greased waxed paper.

Bake at 375 degrees for 13 to 15 minutes or until cake tests done. Invert onto a tea towel sprinkled with confectioners' sugar. Remove the waxed paper. Roll the cake in the towel, starting with the short side. Let stand to cool.

Beat the cream cheese in a mixer bowl until fluffy. Fold in the peaches, 1/2 cup confectioners' sugar and almond flavoring.

Unroll the cake. Spread with the cream cheese mixture. Reroll cake to enclose filling. Chill, covered, until ready to serve. Sprinkle with additional confectioners' sugar just before serving.

Raspberry Frost

Yield: 9 servings

1 cup flour	2 egg whites, at room temperature
1/4 cup packed brown sugar	3/4 cup sugar
1/2 cup chopped walnuts	2 tablespoons lemon juice
1/2 cup (1 stick) butter, melted	1 cup whipping cream
16 ounces frozen raspberries, thawed	

Mix the flour, brown sugar, walnuts and butter in a bowl until crumbly. Spread the mixture onto a baking sheet. Bake at 350 degrees for 20 minutes, stirring occasionally. Sprinkle evenly over the bottom of a 9-inch square baking pan, reserving a small amount for garnish.

Combine the raspberries, egg whites, sugar and lemon juice in a large bowl and beat until stiff. Beat the whipping cream in a mixer bowl until stiff peaks form. Fold into the raspberry mixture. Spoon into the prepared pan. Sprinkle with the reserved crumb mixture. Freeze, covered, for 6 to 12 hours. Remove from the freezer 30 minutes before serving.

Note: See *Editor's Note* on page 58.

Moosehead Lake is the largest body of fresh water within the boundaries of one state.
The Great Salt Lake in Utah is larger in area, but it is not a fresh water lake.

Frosty Strawberry Squares

Yield: 10 to 15 servings

1	cup sifted flour	1	cup sugar
1/4	cup packed brown sugar	2	egg whites
1/2	cup chopped walnuts	2	tablespoons lemon juice
1/2	cup (1 stick) butter, melted	1	cup whipping cream
2	cups sliced fresh strawberries		

Combine the flour, brown sugar, walnuts and butter in a bowl, stirring until the mixture is crumbly. Spread the mixture onto a baking sheet. Bake at 350 degrees for 20 minutes, stirring occasionally. Sprinkle 2/3 of the crumb mixture over the bottom of a 9x13-inch pan, reserving the remaining mixture.

Combine the strawberries, sugar, egg whites and lemon juice in a bowl. Beat at high speed for 10 minutes or until stiff. Beat the whipping cream in a mixer bowl until stiff peaks form. Fold into the strawberry mixture. Spoon into the prepared pan. Sprinkle with the reserved crumb mixture. Freeze, covered, for 6 to 12 hours. Cut into squares. Garnish servings with additional strawberries.

Note: May substitute 1 (10-ounce) package partially thawed frozen sliced strawberries for the fresh strawberries and reduce sugar to 3/4 cup.

Note: See *Editor's Note* on page 58.

Chocolate Bits Pudding

Yield: 5 to 6 servings

2	tablespoons ($1/4$ stick) butter or margarine	$1/8$	teaspoon salt
2	cups milk	2	eggs, lightly beaten
$1/4$	cup sugar	$2^1/2$	cups white bread cubes
$1/2$	teaspoon vanilla extract	$3/4$	cup semisweet chocolate chips

Melt the butter in a saucepan over medium heat. Add the milk and sugar. Cook until the sugar is dissolved, stirring constantly. Remove from the heat. Add the vanilla and salt and mix well.

Stir a small amount of the hot mixture into the eggs; stir the eggs into the hot mixture. Fold in the bread cubes and chocolate chips.

Spoon into a 2-quart baking dish. Place the baking dish in a pan of hot water. Bake at 350 degrees for 1 hour. Serve the pudding with whipped cream.

Baked Fudge Pudding

Yield: 6 servings

1	cup sifted flour	2	tablespoons shortening, melted
1/2	cup sugar	1	teaspoon vanilla extract
2	tablespoons baking cocoa	3/4	cup packed brown sugar
2	teaspoons baking powder	1/4	cup baking cocoa
1/2	teaspoon salt	1 3/4	cups hot water
1/2	cup milk		

Sift the flour, sugar, 2 tablespoons baking cocoa, baking powder and salt together into a bowl. Stir in the milk, melted shortening and vanilla. Spoon into a greased 8-inch square baking pan.

Mix the brown sugar and 1/4 cup baking cocoa in a bowl. Add the hot water and mix well. Pour over the filling.

Bake at 350 degrees for 35 to 40 minutes or until set. Serve immediately with whipped cream.

Lighthouse Lemon Pudding

Yield: 6 servings

1	cup sugar	3	egg yolks
1	tablespoon butter	1	cup milk
2	tablespoons (heaping) flour	3	egg whites, beaten
•	Juice and grated zest of 1 lemon		

Beat the sugar and butter in a mixer bowl until creamy. Mix in the flour, lemon juice, lemon zest, egg yolks and milk. Fold in the egg whites. Spoon into an ungreased soufflé pan or 8-inch square baking dish. Place the baking dish in a pan of hot water. Bake at 400 degrees for 45 minutes.

There are more than 2,000 islands off the Maine coast.

Index

Concert in the
Kitchen

A Medley of Maine Recipes
Orchestrated by Friends of Portland Symphony Orchestra

P.O. Box 722
Portland, Maine 04104-0722
For more information, call (207) 773-6128

Please send me _____ copies of **Concert in the Kitchen** at $23.95 each ...... $ _____

Maine residents add 5.5% sales tax at $1.32 each .... $ _____

Postage and handling $4.00 for first book, $1.50 each additional .... $ _____

Total .... $ _____

_____
Name

_____
Address

_____
City   State   Zip

Method of Payment: [   ] MasterCard   [   ] VISA
                     [   ] Check payable to Concert in the Kitchen

_____
Account Number   Expiration Date

_____
Cardholder Name

_____
Signature

Photocopies will be accepted.